One Dish Favourites

Cataloguing data available from Bibliothèque et Archives nationales du Québec.

11-18

© 2018 Juniper Publishing, a division of Sogides Group Inc., a subsidiary of Quebecor Media Inc. (Montreal, Quebec)

All rights reserved.

Legal deposit: 2018
Bibliothèque et Archives nationales du Québec
Library and Archives Canada

ISBN 978-1-988002-87-3

Printed in Canada

EXCLUSIVE DISTRIBUTOR FOR CANADA & USA

Simon & Schuster Canada
166 King Street East, Suite 300
Toronto ON M5A 1J3

Tel: 647-427-8882
Toll Free: 800-387-0446
Fax: 647-430-9446

simonandschuster.ca
canadianliving.com/books

Government of Quebec – Tax credit for book publishing – Administered by SODEC. **sodec.gouv.qc.ca**

This publisher gratefully acknowledges the support of the Société de développement des enterprises culturelles du Québec.

 Canada Council   Conseil des arts
for the Arts   du Canada

We gratefully acknowledge the support of the Canada Council for the Arts for its publishing program.

We acknowledge the financial support of our publishing activity by the Government of Canada through the Canada Book Fund for our publishing activities.

ART DIRECTOR
Colin Elliott

EDITOR
Martin Zibauer

COPY EDITOR
Ruth Hanley

INDEXER
Lisa Fielding

Canadian Living

THE ESSENTIAL COLLECTION

One Dish Favourites

90+ ALL-IN-ONE MEALS FROM
THE CANADIAN LIVING TEST KITCHEN

JUNIPER
PUBLISHING
A Quebecor Media Corporation

Welcome to the Canadian Living Test Kitchen

In the Test Kitchen, we truly enjoy creating one-dish recipes for Canadian families. We love how a healthy, balanced all-in-one dinner simplifies meal planning and prep, while reducing cleanup. Even better, bringing one dish to the table seems to put everyone at ease. Some of our favourite dishes, the ones we often think of as "comfort food," are one-dish meals, including the flavourful casseroles, skillet suppers and hearty soups in this collection. These meals, shared with friends and family, make us feel warm and comfortable. We love that.

What Does Tested Till Perfect Mean?

Every year, the food specialists in the Canadian Living Test Kitchen work together to produce approximately 500 Tested-Till-Perfect recipes. So what does Tested Till Perfect mean? It means we follow a rigorous process to ensure you'll get the same results in your kitchen as we do in ours.

Here's What We Do:

- In the Test Kitchen, we use the same everyday ingredients and equipment commonly found in kitchens across Canada.

- We start by researching ideas and brainstorming as a team.

- We write up the recipe and go straight into the kitchen to try it out.

- We taste, evaluate and tweak the recipe until we really love it.

- Once developed, each recipe gets handed off to other food specialists for more testing and another tasting session.

- We meticulously test and retest each recipe as many times as it takes to make sure it turns out as perfectly in your kitchen as it does in ours.

- We carefully weigh and measure all ingredients, record the data and send the recipe for nutritional analysis.

- The recipe is then edited and rechecked to ensure all the information is correct and it's ready for you to cook.

TESTED TILL PERFECT

Canadian Living TEST KITCHEN

Sheet Pan Steak
& Potatoes
Page 84

Contents

Smoky Tomato & Lentil Soup

MAKES 6 SERVINGS
HANDS-ON TIME 15 MINUTES
TOTAL TIME 40 MINUTES

In Dutch oven or large heavy-bottomed pot, heat oil over medium heat. Cook chorizo, stirring occasionally, until crisp and beginning to brown, about 4 minutes. Transfer 12 slices to plate. Add garlic, onion and red pepper to pot; cook, stirring occasionally, until softened, about 5 minutes.

Stir in lentils, paprika, salt, pepper and cayenne pepper. Cook, stirring often, until fragrant, about 30 seconds. Add tomatoes and broth; bring to boil. Reduce heat to medium-low; cover and simmer, stirring occasionally, until lentils are tender, about 25 minutes.

Stir in parsley. Divide among bowls; top with reserved chorizo.

NUTRITIONAL INFORMATION PER SERVING about 283 cal, 15 g pro, 13 g total fat (4 g sat. fat), 28 g carb (6 g dietary fibre, 9 g sugar), 22 mg chol, 698 mg sodium, 842 mg potassium. % RDI: 7% calcium, 33% iron, 19% vit A, 147% vit C, 67% folate.

2 tbsp	olive oil
¾ cup	thinly sliced dry-cured chorizo
3	cloves garlic, minced
1	onion, chopped
1	sweet red pepper, chopped
¾ cup	dried green or brown lentils, rinsed
1½ tsp	smoked paprika
½ tsp	each salt and pepper
pinch	cayenne pepper
1	796 ml can plum tomatoes, chopped
1	900 ml pkg no-salt-added chicken broth
1½ cups	parsley leaves, chopped

White Bean & Kale Soup

MAKES 8 SERVINGS
HANDS-ON TIME 15 MINUTES
TOTAL TIME 30 MINUTES

300 g	salami, casings removed, halved lengthwise and thinly sliced crosswise
2	leeks (white and light green parts only), chopped
2	carrots, thinly sliced
3	cloves garlic, minced
1 tbsp	each dried oregano and dried sage
4 cups	sodium-reduced chicken broth
2½ cups	water
2	540 ml cans sodium-reduced cannellini beans, drained and rinsed
6 cups	thinly sliced stemmed kale
2 tbsp	lemon juice (approx)
	shaved Parmesan cheese (optional)
1 tsp	extra-virgin olive oil (optional)

In Dutch oven or large heavy-bottomed pot, cook salami over medium heat until browned, 4 to 6 minutes; using slotted spoon, transfer to bowl. Set aside.

In same pot, cook leeks and carrots until softened, 3 to 5 minutes; stir in garlic, oregano and sage. Add broth and water; bring to boil. Reduce heat, cover and simmer for 10 minutes.

Increase heat to medium; stir in salami, beans and kale. Simmer for 5 minutes. Remove from heat; add lemon juice, adding up to 1 tbsp more lemon juice to taste. Add Parmesan (if using) and drizzle with oil (if using).

NUTRITIONAL INFORMATION PER SERVING about 304 cal, 18 g pro, 15 g total fat (5 g sat. fat), 27 g carb (9 g dietary fibre, 5 g sugar), 30 mg chol, 1,014 mg sodium, 582 mg potassium. % RDI: 10% calcium, 21% iron, 68% vit A, 30% vit C, 33% folate.

TEST KITCHEN TIP

For a vegetarian option, omit the salami, cooking the leeks and carrots in 1 tbsp olive oil and using vegetable broth instead of chicken broth. Add salt and pepper to taste.

Beef Stroganoff Soup

MAKES 4 TO 6 SERVINGS
HANDS-ON TIME 25 MINUTES
TOTAL TIME 25 MINUTES

In Dutch oven or large heavy-bottomed pot, heat oil over medium-high heat. Add carrots, onion, garlic and thyme; cook, stirring, until onion is softened, about 2 minutes. Add beef and mushrooms; cook, stirring and breaking up beef with spoon, until beef is no longer pink, about 3 minutes.

Stir in mustard and Worcestershire sauce; cook until slightly thickened, about 1 minute. Add broth, noodles, salt and pepper; bring to boil. Reduce heat, cover and simmer until noodles are tender, about 6 minutes. Stir in peas and sour cream; cook until heated through, about 1 minute. Sprinkle with parsley.

NUTRITIONAL INFORMATION PER EACH OF 6 SERVINGS about 289 cal, 21 g pro, 16 g total fat (6 g sat. fat), 16 g carb (3 g dietary fibre, 4 g sugar), 58 mg chol, 721 mg sodium, 543 mg potassium. % RDI: 7% calcium, 19% iron, 48% vit A, 8% vit C, 12% folate.

4 tsp	olive oil
2	carrots, diced
1	onion, chopped
2	cloves garlic, minced
2 tsp	dried thyme
450 g	lean ground beef
1	227 g pkg cremini mushrooms, stemmed and sliced
1 tbsp	Dijon mustard
1 tbsp	Worcestershire sauce
1	900 ml pkg sodium-reduced beef broth
1½ cups	broad egg noodles
½ tsp	salt
¼ tsp	pepper
½ cup	frozen peas
⅓ cup	sour cream
2 tbsp	chopped fresh parsley

MAKES 6 TO 8 SERVINGS
HANDS-ON TIME 15 MINUTES
TOTAL TIME 30 MINUTES

Chorizo & Cabbage Soup

2 tsp	olive oil
315 g	dry-cured chorizo sausages (about 2 total), halved lengthwise and thinly sliced crosswise
quarter	head green cabbage, thinly sliced (about 4 cups)
1 tsp	caraway seeds
2	large sweet potatoes, peeled and cubed
1	540 ml can navy beans, drained and rinsed
4 cups	sodium-reduced chicken broth
3 cups	water
1 tsp	chopped fresh thyme

In Dutch oven or large heavy-bottomed pot, heat oil over medium-high heat; cook sausages, stirring often, until crisp, about 5 minutes. Using slotted spoon, transfer to plate. Set aside.

In same pot, stir-fry cabbage and caraway seeds over medium-high heat until cabbage is tender-crisp, about 2 minutes. Scrape into small bowl. Set aside.

In same pot, bring sweet potatoes, beans, broth and water to boil. Reduce heat to medium, partially cover and simmer until sweet potatoes are tender, 12 to 15 minutes.

Ladle 2 cups of the soup into blender and purée until smooth; return to pot. Stir in sausages, cabbage mixture and thyme; cook over medium heat, stirring occasionally, until warmed through, about 5 minutes.

NUTRITIONAL INFORMATION PER EACH OF 8 SERVINGS about 335 cal, 18 g pro, 18 g total fat (7 g sat. fat), 26 g carb (5 g dietary fibre, 5 g sugar), 45 mg chol, 1,106 mg sodium, 558 mg potassium. % RDI: 6% calcium, 14% iron, 95% vit A, 24% vit C, 18% folate.

TEST KITCHEN TIP

Chorizo sausages come in two main varieties. Spanish chorizo (and its Portuguese cousin, chouriço) is a dry-cured pork sausage flavoured with spicy or mild smoked paprika. It's usually sliced or chopped before cooking. You'll find dry-cured chorizo in the deli section. Fresh chorizo is common in Mexican and Latin American dishes; look for it in the meat department of your grocery store alongside other fresh sausages.

Asian-Style Chicken Meatballs
in Ginger Soy Broth

MAKES 4 SERVINGS
HANDS-ON TIME 25 MINUTES
TOTAL TIME 30 MINUTES

MEATBALLS In bowl, combine chicken, bread crumbs, green onions, garlic, ginger and soy sauce. Shape by 2 tbsp into balls; arrange on baking sheet. Refrigerate for 10 minutes.

In large nonstick skillet, heat oil over medium heat; cook meatballs, stirring occasionally, until browned, about 4 minutes.

BROTH Meanwhile, in large saucepan, heat oil over medium-high heat. Add bok choy, carrots and half of the green onions; cook, stirring, until slightly softened, about 3 minutes. Add sliced ginger, garlic and half of the chili pepper; cook, stirring, for 1 minute.

Stir in meatballs, broth and water; bring to boil. Reduce heat to simmer, cover and cook until instant-read thermometer inserted in several meatballs reads 165°F, about 5 minutes. Discard ginger slices. Stir in lime juice, soy sauce and salt.

Divide meatballs among serving bowls; top with broth mixture. Sprinkle with remaining chili pepper and green onions.

NUTRITIONAL INFORMATION PER SERVING about 326 cal, 23 g pro, 21 g total fat (5 g sat. fat), 11 g carb (2 g dietary fibre, 3 g sugar), 87 mg chol, 695 mg sodium, 409 mg potassium. % RDI: 10% calcium, 17% iron, 94% vit A, 38% vit C, 20% folate.

MEATBALLS

450 g	lean ground chicken
⅓ cup	panko or dried bread crumbs
2	green onions, minced
2	cloves garlic, finely grated or pressed
2 tsp	grated fresh ginger
2 tsp	sodium-reduced soy sauce
1 tbsp	olive oil

BROTH

2 tsp	olive oil
3	heads bok choy, quartered
2	carrots, thinly sliced
2	green onions, thinly sliced and divided
2	slices (each ¼ inch thick) fresh ginger
1	clove garlic, finely grated or pressed
1 tbsp	thinly sliced red finger chili pepper, divided
2 cups	sodium-reduced chicken broth
1 cup	water
2 tsp	lime juice
1 tsp	sodium-reduced soy sauce
¼ tsp	salt

TEST KITCHEN TIP

Meatballs will hold their shape better when they're browned in a skillet if they are refrigerated beforehand.

Hearty Meatball & Fennel Soup

MAKES 4 SERVINGS
HANDS-ON TIME 15 MINUTES
TOTAL TIME 25 MINUTES

450 g	extra-lean ground beef
⅓ cup	quick-cooking (not instant) rolled oats
1	egg, lightly beaten
½ tsp	Dijon mustard
½ tsp	each garlic powder, onion powder and dried oregano
¼ tsp	hot pepper flakes
2 tsp	olive oil
1	bulb fennel, trimmed and thinly sliced
1	small onion, finely diced
2	cloves garlic, minced
2 cups	no-salt-added beef broth
2 cups	water
1 cup	bottled strained tomatoes (passata)
½ tsp	pepper
½ tsp	liquid honey
pinch	salt
3 tbsp	chopped fresh parsley
2 tsp	lemon juice

In bowl, stir together beef, oats, egg, mustard, garlic powder, onion powder, oregano and hot pepper flakes until combined. Shape by about 1 tbsp into balls; set aside.

In Dutch oven or large heavy-bottomed pot, heat oil over medium heat; cook fennel and onion, stirring frequently, until beginning to soften, about 5 minutes.

Stir in garlic; cook until fragrant, about 1 minute. Stir in broth, water, strained tomatoes, pepper, honey and salt; bring to boil. Reduce heat and simmer, stirring occasionally, until fennel is tender-crisp, about 8 minutes.

Add meatballs; cook, stirring occasionally, until instant-read thermometer inserted into several meatballs reads 160°F, about 5 minutes. Stir in parsley and lemon juice.

NUTRITIONAL INFORMATION PER SERVING about 303 cal, 28 g pro, 13 g total fat (4 g sat. fat), 17 g carb (3 g dietary fibre, 5 g sugar), 108 mg chol, 310 mg sodium, 806 mg potassium. % RDI: 6% calcium, 34% iron, 6% vit A, 20% vit C, 15% folate.

Thick & Creamy Chicken Noodle Soup

MAKES 4 SERVINGS
HANDS-ON TIME 20 MINUTES
TOTAL TIME 30 MINUTES

In Dutch oven or large heavy-bottomed pot, heat oil over medium heat; cook onion, carrot, celery, garlic, thyme, salt and pepper, stirring occasionally, until softened, about 8 minutes.

Add broth and chicken; bring to boil. Reduce heat, cover and simmer for 2 minutes. Stir in noodles; cover and simmer until chicken is no longer pink inside and noodles are al dente, about 9 minutes.

Remove chicken breasts to cutting board. Using 2 forks, shred into bite-size pieces.

In small bowl, whisk together water, cream and flour until smooth. Whisk into soup; bring to boil. Reduce heat and simmer until slightly thickened, about 2 minutes. Stir in chicken and peas; simmer for 1 minute. Stir in parsley.

NUTRITIONAL INFORMATION PER SERVING about 402 cal, 39 g pro, 10 g total fat (4 g sat. fat), 37 g carb (4 g dietary fibre, 6 g sugar), 92 mg chol, 841 mg sodium, 542 mg potassium. % RDI: 5% calcium, 19% iron, 47% vit A, 18% vit C, 49% folate.

2 tsp	olive oil
1	onion, diced
1	carrot, halved lengthwise and thinly sliced crosswise
1	rib celery, chopped
1	clove garlic, minced
1 tsp	chopped fresh thyme
¼ tsp	each salt and pepper
1	900 ml pkg sodium-reduced chicken broth
2	boneless skinless chicken breasts (about 500 g total)
2 cups	broad egg noodles (such as No Yolks)
1 cup	water
¼ cup	35% cream
3 tbsp	all-purpose flour
1 cup	frozen peas
3 tbsp	chopped fresh parsley

TEST KITCHEN TIP

Check the package directions when buying egg noodles. We use noodles that take about 12 minutes to cook so that they're done at the same time as the chicken. You can adjust the timing by adding the noodles to the broth a few minutes early or late.

Curried Chicken & Lentil Soup With Sweet Potato

MAKES 4 SERVINGS
HANDS-ON TIME 15 MINUTES
TOTAL TIME 30 MINUTES

2 tbsp	olive oil
1	onion, chopped
1	rib celery, diced
2	cloves garlic, minced
2 tsp	curry powder
1 tsp	minced fresh ginger
¼ tsp	each ground coriander, ground cumin and pepper
2	boneless skinless chicken breasts (about 450 g total)
1	900 ml pkg sodium-reduced chicken broth
1	796 ml can no-salt-added diced tomatoes
2 cups	diced, peeled sweet potato (about 1 large)
⅔ cup	dry green lentils, rinsed
¼ cup	chopped fresh cilantro
½ tsp	salt

In large saucepan, heat oil over medium heat; cook onion and celery, stirring occasionally, until softened, about 2 minutes. Add garlic, curry powder, ginger, coriander, cumin and pepper; cook, stirring, until fragrant, about 1 minute. Stir in chicken, broth, tomatoes, sweet potato and lentils; bring to boil. Reduce heat, cover and simmer until lentils are tender, 15 to 20 minutes.

Remove chicken breasts to cutting board; using 2 forks, shred into bite-size pieces. Return chicken to soup. Stir in cilantro and salt.

NUTRITIONAL INFORMATION PER SERVING about 418 cal, 40 g pro, 9 g total fat (1 g sat. fat), 45 g carb (8 g dietary fibre, 14 g sugar), 65 mg chol, 975 mg sodium, 1,350 mg potassium. % RDI: 16% calcium, 40% iron, 119% vit A, 45% vit C, 83% folate.

TEST KITCHEN TIP

To make this soup even quicker to prepare, substitute about 2 cups of leftover shredded cooked chicken and 2 cups cooked and cooled lentils. Just simmer the soup until the sweet potato is fork-tender, about 10 minutes.

Slow Cooker Split Pea & Smoked Turkey Soup

MAKES 8 TO 10 SERVINGS
HANDS-ON TIME 30 MINUTES
COOKING TIME 4 HOURS
TOTAL TIME 4¼ HOURS

In slow cooker, combine carrots, celery, onion, split peas, bay leaves, clove, garlic powder, savory, salt, pepper and water. Arrange turkey over top. Cover and cook on high until peas are tender, about 4 hours.

Transfer turkey to large bowl; let cool slightly.

Meanwhile, remove bay leaves and clove from slow cooker. Using immersion blender, purée soup until almost smooth.

Remove and discard bone and fat from turkey. Using 2 forks, shred into bite-size pieces; stir into soup.

NUTRITIONAL INFORMATION PER EACH OF 10 SERVINGS about 199 cal, 21 g pro, 3 g total fat (1 g sat. fat), 24 g carb (4 g dietary fibre, 4 g sugar), 31 mg chol, 545 mg sodium, 558 mg potassium. % RDI: 3% calcium, 16% iron, 26% vit A, 3% vit C, 33% folate.

2	carrots, diced
2	ribs celery, diced
1	onion, diced
1⅔ cups	yellow split peas
2	bay leaves
1	whole clove
1¼ tsp	garlic powder
¾ tsp	dried savory
½ tsp	salt
¼ tsp	pepper
6 cups	water
1	smoked turkey thigh (about 750 g)

TEST KITCHEN TIP

Turkey thighs have more meat and less sinew than the legs. Look for smoked turkey thighs near the deli counter at the grocery store.

Asian-Style Turkey & Cabbage Noodle Soup

MAKES 6 SERVINGS
HANDS-ON TIME 30 MINUTES
TOTAL TIME 30 MINUTES

1 tbsp	vegetable oil
3	cloves garlic, minced
2 cups	shiitake mushrooms, stemmed and sliced
1	900 ml pkg sodium-reduced chicken broth
3 cups	water
2 cups	shredded cooked turkey
2 cups	finely shredded cabbage
1 cup	frozen corn kernels
1 tbsp	sodium-reduced soy sauce
1 tbsp	lime juice
2 tsp	fish sauce
2 tsp	sesame oil
4	green onions, sliced
2	200 g pkgs fresh udon noodles
⅓ cup	fresh cilantro leaves, torn

In Dutch oven or large heavy-bottomed pot, heat vegetable oil over medium heat; cook garlic, stirring, until fragrant, about 1 minute. Add mushrooms; cook, stirring occasionally, until softened, about 2 minutes. Stir in broth and water; bring to boil. Add turkey and cabbage; reduce heat and simmer, stirring occasionally, until turkey is heated through and cabbage is softened, about 5 minutes.

Add corn; cook until heated through, about 2 minutes. Stir in soy sauce, lime juice, fish sauce, sesame oil and green onions.

Meanwhile, in large pot of boiling water, cook noodles according to package directions; drain and stir into soup. Top with cilantro.

NUTRITIONAL INFORMATION PER SERVING about 358 cal, 23 g pro, 8 g total fat (2 g sat. fat), 48 g carb (2 g dietary fibre, 4 g sugar), 37 mg chol, 755 mg sodium, 363 mg potassium. % RDI: 5% calcium, 13% iron, 2% vit A, 12% vit C, 12% folate.

TEST KITCHEN TIP

This soup is a quick and delicious way to use leftovers from your holiday turkey.

Spicy Korean Tofu Soup

MAKES 6 TO 8 SERVINGS
HANDS-ON TIME 35 MINUTES
TOTAL TIME 35 MINUTES

In Dutch oven or large heavy-bottomed pot, heat oil over medium heat; cook onion, stirring occasionally, until softened, about 4 minutes. Add kimchi, garlic and red pepper powder; cook, stirring occasionally, until fragrant, about 4 minutes.

Pour in broth and water; bring to boil. Stir in mushrooms and green onions; reduce heat and simmer, stirring occasionally, until mushrooms are beginning to soften, about 5 minutes. Add zucchini; cook, stirring occasionally, until zucchini are tender-crisp, about 5 minutes.

Using spoon, scoop tofu into scant ¼-cup portions; add to soup. Gently stir in fish sauce and soy sauce; cook until tofu is heated through, about 3 minutes.

Bring to gentle boil; stir in eggs, breaking up yolks. Continue to cook, without stirring, until egg whites are opaque, about 2 minutes.

NUTRITIONAL INFORMATION PER EACH OF 8 SERVINGS about 103 cal, 7 g pro, 5 g total fat (1 g sat. fat), 7 g carb (2 g dietary fibre, 4 g sugar), 69 mg chol, 552 mg sodium, 315 mg potassium. % RDI: 4% calcium, 10% iron, 14% vit A, 17% vit C, 13% folate.

1 tbsp	vegetable oil
½ cup	diced onion (about half onion)
1 cup	kimchi, coarsely chopped
2	cloves garlic, minced
1 tbsp	Korean red pepper powder (gochugaru)
2 cups	sodium-reduced chicken broth or vegetable broth
2 cups	water
1 cup	thinly sliced shiitake mushrooms
3	green onions, thinly sliced
2	zucchini, halved lengthwise and thinly sliced crosswise
1	510 g pkg soft silken or soft tofu, drained
1 tbsp	fish sauce
1 tsp	sodium-reduced soy sauce
3	eggs

TEST KITCHEN TIP

Korean red pepper powder, or gochugaru, has a sweet, fruity and slightly smoky flavour and is a key ingredient in kimchi. It's different than other ground chilies and is worth finding to give this soup authentic Korean flavour; look for it in major grocery stores and Asian markets.

Slow Cooker Corn & Smoked Ham Chowder

MAKES 8 SERVINGS
HANDS-ON TIME 25 MINUTES
COOKING TIME 8½ HOURS
TOTAL TIME 8¾ HOURS

CHOWDER

6 cups	frozen corn kernels
2 cups	cubed smoked boneless ham
2	ribs celery, diced
1	onion, diced
1	sweet green pepper, diced
1	jalapeño pepper, seeded and minced
2	cloves garlic, minced
2	bay leaves
1 tbsp	Cajun or Creole seasoning
1½ tsp	dried thyme
½ tsp	each salt and pepper
2 cups	sodium-reduced chicken broth
2 cups	water
1 cup	milk
3 tbsp	cornstarch

PAPRIKA & CHIVE CREMA

¾ cup	sour cream
¼ cup	chopped fresh chives
1 tsp	sweet or smoked paprika
¼ tsp	pepper

CHOWDER In slow cooker, combine corn, ham, celery, onion, green pepper, jalapeño pepper, garlic, bay leaves, Cajun seasoning, thyme, salt and pepper. Stir in broth and water. Cover and cook on low for 8 hours.

Discard bay leaves. Whisk milk with cornstarch; whisk into slow cooker. Cover and cook on high until slightly thickened, about 30 minutes.

PAPRIKA & CHIVE CREMA Meanwhile, in small bowl, stir together sour cream, chives, paprika and pepper. Set aside.

Turn off slow cooker. Using immersion blender, purée soup until slightly smooth with some chunks remaining, about 20 seconds. Ladle into serving bowls; top with crema.

NUTRITIONAL INFORMATION PER SERVING about 237 cal, 16 g pro, 7 g total fat (3 g sat. fat), 33 g carb (4 g dietary fibre, 7 g sugar), 29 mg chol, 835 mg sodium, 581 mg potassium. % RDI: 9% calcium, 12% iron, 12% vit A, 32% vit C, 25% folate.

TEST KITCHEN TIP

To make your own Cajun seasoning, combine ¼ cup each paprika and dried parsley; 2 tbsp each garlic powder and dried oregano and thyme; 1 tsp salt; and ½ tsp cayenne pepper. Store in airtight container at room temperature in dark place for up to 1 month. Makes about ¾ cup.

The Ultimate Clam Chowder

MAKES 8 SERVINGS
HANDS-ON TIME 45 MINUTES
TOTAL TIME 1¼ HOURS

Scrub clams; discard any that do not close when tapped. In Dutch oven or large heavy-bottomed pot, bring clams and water to boil over high heat. Reduce heat to medium; cover and cook until most clams have opened, about 10 minutes.

Using a slotted spoon, transfer opened clams to a bowl and set aside. Continue to cook unopened clams, covered, for an additional 2 minutes, then stir. Discard any that remain closed.

Strain cooking liquid through cheesecloth-lined fine-mesh sieve into bowl; pour into liquid measure. Add enough water to yield 3½ cups. Set aside.

Remove meat from all but 8 of the clams; coarsely chop meat. Refrigerate chopped clam meat and remaining clams until ready to use.

In Dutch oven or large heavy-bottomed pot, cook bacon over medium heat, stirring often, until crisp, about 10 minutes. Using slotted spoon, transfer bacon to paper towel–lined plate; set aside.

Drain all but 2 tbsp fat from pot. Add butter; melt over medium heat. Cook shallots and celery, stirring occasionally, until softened, about 8 minutes. Add garlic, thyme and bay leaf; cook, stirring frequently, until fragrant, about 1 minute. Sprinkle with flour; cook, stirring frequently, for 1 minute.

Gradually whisk in reserved cooking liquid. Stir in potatoes and pepper; bring to boil. Reduce heat; cover and simmer, stirring occasionally, until potatoes are fork-tender, about 20 minutes.

Discard thyme and bay leaf. Stir in sherry, lemon juice and Worcestershire sauce; bring to simmer. Cook, stirring occasionally, for 5 minutes. Stir in cream, chopped clam meat and bacon; cook until heated through, about 3 minutes. Stir in chives and parsley. Ladle into serving bowls; top with reserved clams.

2.25 kg	fresh littleneck clams
1 cup	water
6	strips bacon, diced
1 tbsp	butter
2	shallots, diced
1	rib celery, diced
2	cloves garlic, minced
2	sprigs fresh thyme
1	bay leaf
⅓ cup	all-purpose flour
550 g	yellow-fleshed potatoes (about 2), peeled and diced
½ tsp	pepper
½ cup	dry sherry
1 tbsp	lemon juice
1 tsp	Worcestershire sauce
1½ cups	18% cream
2 tbsp	each chopped fresh chives and fresh parsley

NUTRITIONAL INFORMATION PER SERVING about 292 cal, 12 g pro, 16 g total fat (8 g sat. fat), 23 g carb (1 g dietary fibre, 3 g sugar), 60 mg chol, 437 mg sodium, 653 mg potassium. % RDI: 9% calcium, 56% iron, 15% vit A, 22% vit C, 13% folate.

Pumpkin Soba Noodle Soup

MAKES 4 SERVINGS
HANDS-ON TIME 30 MINUTES
TOTAL TIME 30 MINUTES

225 g	soba noodles
1 tbsp	each sesame oil and salted butter
2	cloves garlic, minced
1 tbsp	grated fresh ginger
1 cup	thinly sliced shiitake mushrooms
4 cups	sodium-reduced vegetable or mushroom broth
3 tbsp	hoisin sauce
2 tbsp	sodium-reduced soy sauce
1 tbsp	rice vinegar
3 cups	cubed peeled pumpkin or butternut squash
1½ cups	frozen shelled edamame
4 cups	packed baby spinach

In large pot of boiling salted water, cook noodles according to package directions. Drain and rinse under warm water; drain well. Set aside.

Meanwhile, in large saucepan, heat sesame oil and butter over medium heat; cook garlic and ginger for 1 minute. Add mushrooms; cook, stirring often, until softened, about 8 minutes. Add broth, hoisin sauce, soy sauce and vinegar. Bring to boil; add pumpkin. Reduce heat to medium; partially cover and simmer until pumpkin is tender, about 15 minutes. Add edamame during last 5 minutes of cooking. Remove from heat; stir in spinach. Divide noodles among serving bowls; ladle soup over top.

NUTRITIONAL INFORMATION PER SERVING about 416 cal, 19 g pro, 10 g total fat (3 g sat. fat), 71 g carb (11 g dietary fibre, 9 g sugar), 8 mg chol, 988 mg sodium, 835 mg potassium. % RDI: 14% calcium, 34% iron, 149% vit A, 37% vit C, 104% folate.

TEST KITCHEN TIP

Be sure not to confuse seasoned rice vinegar, which has added sugar and salt, with unseasoned rice vinegar. If we don't specify seasoned rice vinegar in our recipes, you should use unseasoned.

Hearty Beef Stew

MAKES 6 TO 8 SERVINGS
HANDS-ON TIME 15 MINUTES
COOKING TIME 8¼ HOURS
TOTAL TIME 8½ HOURS

BEEF STEW Sprinkle beef with salt and pepper; place in slow cooker. Add carrots, onion, garlic, mushrooms, thyme and bay leaves.

Whisk together broth, wine, tomato paste, cocoa powder and Worcestershire sauce; pour over beef. Cover and cook on low until beef is tender, about 8 hours. Skim fat from surface of cooking liquid.

Discard thyme and bay leaves. Whisk cornstarch with water until smooth; stir into slow cooker. Cover and cook on high until thickened, about 15 minutes.

GREMOLATA Meanwhile, in small bowl, stir together parsley, lemon zest and garlic. Serve over mashed potatoes; sprinkle with Gremolata.

NUTRITIONAL INFORMATION PER EACH OF 8 SERVINGS about 305 cal, 35 g pro, 13 g total fat (5 g sat. fat), 12 g carb (2 g dietary fibre, 3 g sugar), 94 mg chol, 762 mg sodium, 705 mg potassium. % RDI: 4% calcium, 30% iron, 32% vit A, 17% vit C, 10% folate.

BEEF STEW

1.35 kg	beef stewing cubes, cut in 1½-inch chunks
1½ tsp	salt
1 tsp	pepper
4	carrots, coarsely chopped
1	onion, chopped
3	cloves garlic, finely grated or pressed
1	14 g pkg dried mixed mushrooms
3	sprigs fresh thyme
2	bay leaves
2½ cups	sodium-reduced beef broth
½ cup	dry red wine
3 tbsp	tomato paste
2 tsp	cocoa powder
1 tsp	Worcestershire sauce
¼ cup	cornstarch
¼ cup	water

GREMOLATA

½ cup	chopped fresh parsley
2 tsp	grated lemon zest
1	clove garlic, finely grated or pressed

TEST KITCHEN TIP

If you want to avoid washing another pot, prepare rustic smashed potatoes in the slow cooker. Add 675 g of halved mini potatoes to the slow cooker with the stew. Using slotted spoon, remove potatoes; coarsely mash.

MAKES 8 TO 10 SERVINGS
HANDS-ON TIME 15 MINUTES
COOKING TIME 8¼ HOURS
TOTAL TIME 8¼ HOURS

Slow Cooker Japanese-Style Beef Curry

900 g	beef stewing cubes, cut in 1-inch chunks
2½ cups	sodium-reduced beef broth
2	large white potatoes (about 450 g total), peeled and cut in 1-inch chunks
1	sweet onion, finely chopped
2	ribs celery, thinly sliced
1	large carrot, cut in ½-inch thick rounds
¼ cup	mild curry powder
¼ cup	tomato paste
3 tbsp	granulated sugar
3 tbsp	sodium-reduced soy sauce
2 tbsp	Worcestershire sauce
3	star anise
2	bay leaves
4	cloves garlic, minced
4 tsp	minced fresh ginger
1 tsp	salt
¼ tsp	each pepper and five-spice powder
¼ cup	all-purpose flour
3 tbsp	water
2 tbsp	unsalted butter, melted
1 tbsp	vinegar

In slow cooker, combine beef, broth, potatoes, onion, celery, carrot, curry powder, tomato paste, sugar, soy sauce, Worcestershire sauce, star anise, bay leaves, garlic, ginger, salt, pepper and five-spice powder. Cover and cook on low until beef is tender, 8 to 9 hours.

Whisk together flour, water and butter until smooth; stir into slow cooker. Cover and cook on high until thickened, about 15 minutes. Stir in vinegar; discard bay leaves and star anise.

NUTRITIONAL INFORMATION PER EACH OF 10 SERVINGS about 256 cal, 22 g pro, 9 g total fat (4 g sat. fat), 22 g carb (3 g dietary fibre, 8 g sugar), 55 mg chol, 679 mg sodium, 644 mg potassium. % RDI: 4% calcium, 25% iron, 20% vit A, 12% vit C, 12% folate.

TEST KITCHEN TIP

If you prefer a spicier curry, use a hot curry powder, such as Madras-style curry powder, or add ground chilies to taste.

Braised Chinese Beef & Daikon With Noodles

MAKES 8 SERVINGS
HANDS-ON TIME 40 MINUTES
COOKING TIME 3 HOURS
TOTAL TIME 3¾ HOURS

In large bowl, stir together 2 tbsp of the flour, the coriander, pepper, five-spice powder and salt; add beef and toss to coat.

In Dutch oven or large heavy-bottomed pot, heat oil over medium-high heat; working in batches, cook brisket, stirring, until browned, about 5 minutes. Transfer to plate. Add garlic and ginger to pot; cook over medium-high heat, stirring, until fragrant, about 30 seconds. Stir in wine, scraping up browned bits. Add broth, sugar, star anise, cinnamon stick, beef mixture and ¾ cup water; bring to boil. Reduce heat; cover and simmer until beef is tender, about 2½ hours.

Stir in daikon; bring to boil. Reduce heat and simmer, uncovered, until daikon is tender, about 30 minutes.

Meanwhile, whisk together oyster sauce, remaining 2 tbsp flour and 1 tbsp water; stir into beef mixture. Cook, stirring, until sauce is thickened, about 5 minutes. Stir in green onions; cook for 1 minute.

Meanwhile, in large pot of boiling water, cook noodles according to package directions; drain. Serve topped with beef mixture.

NUTRITIONAL INFORMATION PER SERVING about 652 cal, 33 g pro, 27 g total fat (9 g sat. fat), 70 g carb (3 g dietary fibre, 3 g sugar), 92 mg chol, 491 mg sodium, 480 mg potassium. % RDI: 5% calcium, 48% iron, 1% vit A, 12% vit C, 10% folate.

¼ cup	all-purpose flour, divided
2 tsp	ground coriander
½ tsp	pepper
¼ tsp	five-spice powder
pinch	salt
900 g	boneless beef brisket pot roast, cut in 1-inch chunks
2 tbsp	vegetable oil
6	cloves garlic, minced
1 tbsp	minced fresh ginger
¼ cup	Chinese rice wine
1½ cups	sodium-reduced beef broth
1 tsp	granulated sugar
2	star anise
1	cinnamon stick (3½ inches long)
¾ cup	water, divided (approx)
340 g	daikon radish, peeled and cut in 1-inch chunks (about 4½ cups)
2 tbsp	oyster sauce
4	green onions, cut in 1½-inch lengths
680 g	fresh steamed chow mein noodles or fresh Chinese wheat noodles

TEST KITCHEN TIP

Look for daikon—a large, long white Asian radish—in the produce section of your grocery store. If it's not available, use white turnip instead; both have a similar flavour when cooked.

MAKES 8 SERVINGS
HANDS-ON TIME 20 MINUTES
TOTAL TIME 1½ HOURS

Western Chili

2 tbsp	vegetable oil
2	onions, finely chopped
2	cloves garlic, finely grated or pressed
2 tsp	ground cumin
900 g	lean ground beef
1	796 ml can whole tomatoes
3 tbsp	chili powder
2 tsp	each dried oregano, granulated sugar and sweet paprika
1 tsp	cocoa powder
1 tsp	salt
½ tsp	pepper
1	bay leaf
1	540 ml can red kidney beans, drained and rinsed

In Dutch oven or large heavy- bottomed pot, heat oil over medium-high heat; cook onions and garlic, stirring frequently, until onions are softened, about 5 minutes.

Add cumin; cook, stirring, until fragrant, about 1 minute. Add beef; cook, stirring and breaking up with spoon, until no longer pink, about 5 minutes. Stir in tomatoes, breaking up with spoon.

Stir in chili powder, oregano, sugar, paprika, cocoa powder, salt, pepper and bay leaf; bring to boil. Reduce heat; partially cover and simmer, stirring occasionally, for 1 hour. Discard bay leaf.

Stir in beans; cook until heated through, about 3 minutes. *(Make-ahead: Cover and refrigerate for up to 24 hours. Reheat before serving.)*

NUTRITIONAL INFORMATION PER SERVING about 360 cal, 27 g pro, 20 g total fat (7 g sat. fat), 19 g carb (6 g dietary fibre, 6 g sugar), 67 mg chol, 688 mg sodium, 754 mg potassium. % RDI: 8% calcium, 34% iron, 12% vit A, 30% vit C, 20% folate.

TEST KITCHEN TIP

Customize your chili with the toppings you serve. We chose sour cream, shredded cheese, chopped cilantro and diced cucumber. You can also include diced avocado, tortilla chips, chopped fresh tomatoes and sliced green onions.

Beef & Okra Stew

Sweet & Sour Beef Stew
With Prunes & Apricots
Page 38

Beef & Okra Stew

MAKES 6 SERVINGS
HANDS-ON TIME 30 MINUTES
TOTAL TIME 2¾ HOURS

In Dutch oven or large heavy-bottomed pot, heat 1 tbsp of the oil over medium heat; cook red onion and celery, stirring occasionally, until softened, about 8 minutes. Scrape into bowl.

Add remaining 1 tbsp oil to pot; heat over medium-high heat. Working in batches, cook beef, stirring, until browned, about 7 minutes. Transfer to plate. Add chorizo and garlic to pot; cook, stirring, for 1 minute. Stir in onion mixture and flour; cook, stirring, until flour is golden, about 3 minutes.

Stir in broth, water, Cajun seasoning, paprika and pepper; return beef and any accumulated juices to pot. Bring to boil; cover, reduce heat and simmer for 1 hour. Uncover and cook, stirring occasionally, until beef is tender, 1 to 1½ hours.

Stir in red pepper and okra; cook, stirring occasionally, until red pepper is tender, about 30 minutes. *(Make-ahead: Let cool for 30 minutes. Refrigerate in airtight container for up to 3 days or freeze for up to 1 month.)*

Top with green onions.

NUTRITIONAL INFORMATION PER SERVING about 557 cal, 44 g pro, 36 g total fat (13 g sat. fat), 14 g carb (3 g dietary fibre, 5 g sugar), 125 mg chol, 959 mg sodium, 838 mg potassium. % RDI: 7% calcium, 34% iron, 17% vit A, 67% vit C, 20% folate.

2 tbsp	vegetable oil, divided
1	red onion, chopped
1	rib celery, chopped
900 g	stewing beef cubes
1	250 g pkg mild dry-cured chorizo, sliced
2	cloves garlic, minced
3 tbsp	all-purpose flour
3 cups	sodium-reduced chicken broth
1 cup	water
2 tsp	Cajun seasoning (see Tip, page 24)
1½ tsp	smoked paprika
¼ tsp	pepper
1	sweet red pepper, chopped
2 cups	okra (about 180 g), chopped
2	green onions, thinly sliced

TEST KITCHEN TIP

Okra acts as a natural thickener in this gumbo-style stew. If you can't find fresh okra, use frozen instead.

Sweet & Sour Beef Stew
With Prunes & Apricots

Page 36

MAKES 10 SERVINGS
HANDS-ON TIME 35 MINUTES
TOTAL TIME 3 HOURS

1 tbsp	vegetable oil, divided
2	onions, thinly sliced
2	ribs celery, thinly sliced
1.35 kg	beef stewing cubes
½ tsp	each salt and pepper
2	cloves garlic, minced
2 tsp	ground ginger
½ tsp	each cinnamon and ground allspice
2	bay leaves
3 cups	sodium-reduced beef broth
1 cup	dry red wine
⅓ cup	cider vinegar
2 tbsp	packed brown sugar
2 tsp	Worcestershire sauce
4	carrots, chopped
2	white turnips, peeled and cubed
½ cup	pitted prunes, chopped
½ cup	dried apricots, chopped
2 tbsp	all-purpose flour
2 tbsp	cold water

In Dutch oven or large heavy-bottomed pot, heat 1 tsp of the oil over medium heat; cook onions and celery until softened, about 7 minutes. Scrape into bowl.

Toss together beef, salt and pepper. In same pot, heat remaining 2 tsp oil over medium-high heat; working in batches and stirring occasionally, cook beef until browned, about 6 minutes. Add garlic; cook, stirring, about 1 minute. Add onion mixture, ginger, cinnamon, allspice and bay leaves; cook, stirring, for 1 minute. Stir in broth, wine, vinegar, brown sugar and Worcestershire sauce; bring to boil. Reduce heat, cover and simmer for 1½ hours.

Add carrots, turnips, prunes and apricots; cook until turnips are tender, about 45 minutes. Discard bay leaves.

Whisk flour with cold water; whisk into stew. Simmer until slightly thickened, about 10 minutes.

NUTRITIONAL INFORMATION PER SERVING about 341 cal, 29 g pro, 15 g total fat (6 g sat. fat), 22 g carb (3 g dietary fibre, 13 g sugar), 80 mg chol, 452 mg sodium, 778 mg potassium. % RDI: 6% calcium, 26% iron, 54% vit A, 13% vit C, 10% folate.

Slow Cooker Pork & Grainy Mustard Stew

MAKES 8 SERVINGS
HANDS-ON TIME 15 MINUTES
TOTAL TIME 1½ HOURS

Toss pork with 1 tbsp of the flour. In Dutch oven or large heavy-bottomed pot, heat 1½ tbsp of the oil over medium-high heat; working in batches and adding more oil as needed, cook pork, stirring, until browned, about 5 minutes. Transfer to plate.

In same pot, heat remaining 1½ tbsp oil. Add onions, carrots, celery, garlic, thyme, salt and pepper; cook, stirring occasionally, until softened, about 5 minutes.

Add broth, water, wine and bay leaf; return pork and any accumulated juices to pot. Bring to boil; reduce heat, cover and simmer, stirring occasionally, for about 45 minutes or until meat is tender. Discard bay leaf.

Whisk together mustard, water and remaining 1 tbsp flour; stir into stew and simmer until thickened, 3 minutes. Stir in peas and parsley; heat through, 3 minutes. *(Make-ahead: Let cool for 30 minutes; refrigerate, uncovered, in shallow container until cold. Cover and refrigerate for up to 3 days. Or freeze for up to 1 month; thaw in refrigerator.)*

NUTRITIONAL INFORMATION PER SERVING about 315 cal, 37 g pro, 13 g total fat (3 g sat. fat), 11 g carb (2 g dietary fibre), 109 mg chol, 480 mg sodium. % RDI: 5% calcium, 23% iron, 69% vit A, 12% vit C, 15% folate.

3 lb	boneless pork shoulder blade roast, trimmed and cubed
2 tbsp	all-purpose flour, divided
3 tbsp	vegetable oil, divided (approx)
2	onions, chopped
4	carrots, chopped
2	ribs celery, chopped
2	cloves garlic, minced
1 tsp	dried thyme
¼ tsp	each salt and pepper
2 cups	sodium-reduced chicken broth
1½ cups	water
½ cup	white wine or sodium-reduced chicken broth
1	bay leaf
¼ cup	grainy mustard
2 tbsp	water
¾ cup	frozen green peas
¼ cup	minced fresh parsley

Slow Cooker Tomato Fennel Pork Stew

MAKES 4 SERVINGS
HANDS-ON TIME 30 MINUTES
COOKING TIME 6¼ HOURS
TOTAL TIME 6½ HOURS

900 g	boneless pork shoulder blade roast
½ tsp	each salt and pepper, divided
2 tbsp	vegetable oil, divided (approx)
1	onion, chopped
2	carrots, chopped
2	ribs celery, chopped
4	cloves garlic
2 tsp	fennel seeds, crushed
½ cup	sodium-reduced chicken broth
2 cups	bottled strained tomatoes (passata)
3	sprigs fresh thyme (or 1 tsp dried thyme)
1 tbsp	all-purpose flour
2 tbsp	water
⅓ cup	chopped pitted black olives
¼ cup	chopped fresh parsley

Trim pork; cut into 1-inch cubes. Sprinkle with ¼ tsp each of the salt and pepper. In Dutch oven or large heavy-bottomed pot, heat 1 tbsp of the oil over medium-high heat; working in batches and adding more oil if necessary, cook pork, stirring, until browned, about 5 minutes. Transfer to slow cooker.

Drain fat from pot; add remaining 1 tbsp oil. Add onion, carrots, celery, garlic, fennel seeds and remaining ¼ tsp each salt and pepper; cook over medium heat, stirring often, until onions are softened and lightly golden, 8 minutes. Add broth, stirring and scraping up any browned bits. Add to slow cooker.

Add strained tomatoes and thyme to slow cooker. Cover and cook on low for 6 to 7 hours.

Whisk flour with water until smooth; whisk into slow cooker. Stir in olives; cover and cook on high until thickened, 15 minutes. Stir in parsley.

NUTRITIONAL INFORMATION PER SERVING about 355 cal, 37 g pro, 15 g total fat (3 g sat. fat), 17 g carb (3 g dietary fibre), 104 mg chol, 640 mg sodium. % RDI: 10% calcium, 36% iron, 77% vit A, 33% vit C, 18% folate.

Slow Cooker Jamaican Curried Lamb

MAKES 8 SERVINGS
HANDS-ON TIME 15 MINUTES
COOKING TIME 8¼ HOURS
TOTAL TIME 8¼ HOURS

In slow cooker, combine lamb, coconut milk, onion, tomato paste, Scotch bonnet pepper, curry powder, dried thyme, ginger, soy sauce, garlic, allspice and salt.

Cover and cook on low until lamb is tender, 8 to 9 hours.

Skim any fat from surface of cooking liquid. Whisk flour with water until smooth; stir into slow cooker. Cover and cook on high until thickened, about 15 minutes. Garnish with fresh thyme (if using).

NUTRITIONAL INFORMATION PER SERVING about 401 cal, 27 g pro, 17 g total fat (12 g sat. fat), 9 g carb (2 g dietary fibre, 2 g sugar), 84 mg chol, 328 mg sodium, 649 mg potassium. % RDI: 6% calcium, 37% iron, 2% vit A, 7% vit C, 20% folate.

1 kg	boneless lamb shoulder, cut in 1-inch chunks
1	400 ml can coconut milk
1	onion, cut in 1-inch chunks
3 tbsp	tomato paste
1	Scotch bonnet pepper, seeded and chopped
2 tbsp	curry powder
2 tbsp	dried thyme
2 tbsp	minced fresh ginger
2 tbsp	sodium-reduced soy sauce
3	cloves garlic, minced
2 tsp	ground allspice
¼ tsp	salt
2 tbsp	all-purpose flour
3 tbsp	water
2 tsp	fresh thyme leaves (optional)

TEST KITCHEN TIP

For a more authentic Jamaican stew, you can replace the lamb with 1.35 kg cubed bone-in goat or mutton. You can find goat and mutton at Caribbean and Middle Eastern butcher shops and some larger supermarkets.

Scotch bonnet peppers (a variety very similar to habanero) are among the hottest you'll find in grocery stores. Wear disposable gloves when you prep them, and reduce the amount if you don't like a spicy curry.

Chicken & Wild Mushroom Stew

MAKES 4 TO 6 SERVINGS
HANDS-ON TIME 15 MINUTES
TOTAL TIME 6½ HOURS

4 cups	button mushrooms, halved
2	shallots, thinly sliced
1	14 g pkg dried chanterelle mushrooms or dried mixed mushrooms, chopped
1 tbsp	dried thyme
1 tsp	salt
½ tsp	pepper
8	bone-in chicken thighs, skin removed
1 cup	sodium-reduced chicken broth
1 cup	dry white wine (such as Sauvignon Blanc)
2 tbsp	grainy mustard
¼ cup	cornstarch
¼ cup	10% cream
2 tsp	white wine vinegar
¼ cup	lightly packed fresh tarragon leaves or microgreens

In slow cooker, combine button mushrooms, shallots, chanterelle mushrooms, thyme, salt and pepper; arrange chicken over top.

Whisk together broth, wine and mustard; pour over chicken. Cover and cook on low until juices run clear when thickest part is pierced, 6 to 8 hours.

Whisk together cornstarch, cream and vinegar until smooth; pour into slow cooker. Cover and cook on high until thickened, about 15 minutes.

Garnish with tarragon. Serve with steamed rice or mashed potatoes.

NUTRITIONAL INFORMATION PER EACH OF 6 SERVINGS about 262 cal, 34 g pro, 8 g total fat (3 g sat. fat), 12 g carb (2 g dietary fibre, 3 g sugar), 152 mg chol, 710 mg sodium, 660 mg potassium. % RDI: 5% calcium, 20% iron, 4% vit A, 2% vit C, 9% folate.

TEST KITCHEN TIP

Chicken thighs are well-suited to stews, braises and other slow-cooking dishes. Thighs have more flavour than breast meat; they also stay moist and tender during the long cooking time.

Quick Chicken & White Bean Stew

MAKES 4 SERVINGS
HANDS-ON TIME 25 MINUTES
TOTAL TIME 30 MINUTES

In Dutch oven or large heavy-bottomed pot, cook bacon over medium heat, stirring, until lightly crisp, about 3 minutes.

Add chicken; cook, stirring, until browned, about 4 minutes. Using slotted spoon, transfer mixture to plate; set aside.

In same pot, heat oil over medium heat; cook onion, stirring, until softened, about 3 minutes. Add garlic and thyme; cook, stirring, until fragrant, about 1 minute. Add mushrooms and 2 tbsp of the water; cook, stirring occasionally and scraping up browned bits, until mushrooms are tender and no liquid remains, 4 to 5 minutes.

Return chicken mixture and any juices to pot. Stir in beans, strained tomatoes, salt, pepper and remaining ½ cup water; bring to boil. Reduce heat, cover and simmer until stew is slightly thickened and chicken is no longer pink inside, about 8 minutes. Remove from heat; stir in green onions, parsley and vinegar.

NUTRITIONAL INFORMATION PER SERVING about 449 cal, 35 g pro, 14 g total fat (5 g sat. fat), 45 g carb (10 g dietary fibre, 8 g sugar), 101 mg chol, 418 mg sodium, 1,204 mg potassium. % RDI: 11% calcium, 48% iron, 4% vit A, 18% vit C, 40% folate.

2	strips bacon, thinly sliced
450 g	boneless skinless chicken thighs, quartered
2 tsp	vegetable oil
1	onion, sliced
6	cloves garlic, sliced
1 tbsp	chopped fresh thyme
1	227 g pkg cremini or button mushrooms, sliced
⅔ cup	water, divided (approx)
1	540 ml can navy beans, drained and rinsed
2 cups	bottled strained tomatoes (passata)
pinch	each salt and pepper
2	green onions, sliced
2 tbsp	chopped fresh parsley
1 tsp	red wine vinegar

Cider-Braised Chicken Thighs
With Smashed Potatoes

MAKES 4 SERVINGS
HANDS-ON TIME 15 MINUTES
TOTAL TIME 30 MINUTES

CIDER-BRAISED CHICKEN

4	bone-in skin-on chicken thighs (about 450 g total)
½ tsp	each salt and pepper, divided
4 tsp	olive oil, divided
2	Gala apples, cored and cut in ½-inch thick wedges
1	small onion, chopped
2	cloves garlic, finely chopped
2	sprigs fresh thyme
½ cup	dry hard cider
¾ cup	sodium-reduced chicken broth
2 tsp	Dijon mustard
2 tsp	all-purpose flour
1 tbsp	water

SMASHED POTATOES

800 g	red-skinned potatoes, scrubbed and cut in 1-inch chunks
½ cup	milk
2 tbsp	butter
1 tbsp	fresh thyme leaves
pinch	each salt and pepper

CIDER-BRAISED CHICKEN Sprinkle chicken with ¼ tsp each of the salt and pepper. In Dutch oven or large heavy-bottomed pot, heat 2 tsp of the oil over medium-high heat; cook chicken until browned, about 6 minutes. Transfer to plate. Set aside.

In same pot, heat 1 tsp of the remaining oil over medium-high heat; cook apples, turning once, until golden, about 2 minutes. Transfer to separate plate. Set aside.

In same pot, heat remaining 1 tsp oil over medium-high heat; cook onion, garlic and thyme, stirring, until softened, about 2 minutes. Pour in cider; cook, scraping up browned bits, until slightly reduced, about 1 minute.

Stir in broth, mustard and remaining ¼ tsp each of the salt and pepper; bring to boil. Add chicken and any accumulated juices. Reduce heat, cover and simmer until juices run clear when thickest part of chicken is pierced, about 18 minutes.

Transfer chicken to clean plate. Discard thyme. Whisk flour with water; add to sauce and cook, stirring, until slightly thickened, about 2 minutes. Stir in apples.

SMASHED POTATOES Meanwhile, in large pot of boiling salted water, cook potatoes until fork-tender, about 15 minutes; drain and return to pot. Cook over medium heat, stirring, for 1 minute. Add milk, butter, thyme, salt and pepper; coarsely mash together. Serve with apple mixture and chicken.

NUTRITIONAL INFORMATION PER SERVING about 566 cal, 22 g pro, 30 g total fat (10 g sat. fat), 51 g carb (6 g dietary fibre, 14 g sugar), 98 mg chol, 1,047 mg sodium, 1,215 mg potassium. % RDI: 9% calcium, 21% iron, 11% vit A, 58% vit C, 20% folate.

TEST KITCHEN TIP

In the grocery store, look for potatoes that are firm and free of bruising. Avoid any with a green tint; they've been overexposed to light and are producing a chemical that can, in large amounts, make you ill.

Store your potatoes in a cool, dark place between 7°C and 10°C. Avoid storing potatoes near onions, which produce a gas that encourages potatoes to sprout.

Spanish Chicken Stew

MAKES 10 SERVINGS
HANDS-ON TIME 35 MINUTES
TOTAL TIME 50 MINUTES

In Dutch oven or large heavy-bottomed pot, heat oil over high heat; working in batches, cook chicken until browned, about 6 minutes. Remove from pot and set aside.

Add leeks and garlic to pot; cook over medium-high heat until garlic is fragrant, about 1 minute.

Return chicken to pot; cook, stirring frequently, until leeks begin to soften, about 4 minutes.

Add red peppers, tomato paste and salt; cook, stirring, for 2 minutes. Stir in tomatoes, breaking up with wooden spoon; bring to boil. Reduce heat and simmer for 10 minutes.

Meanwhile, in large pot of boiling lightly salted water, cook potatoes just until fork-tender, about 8 minutes. Drain potatoes and add to stew; simmer until stew is thickened, about 15 minutes.

Stir in peas and parsley; cook until peas are warmed through, about 2 minutes.

NUTRITIONAL INFORMATION PER SERVING about 218 cal, 21 g pro, 5 g total fat (1 g sat. fat), 23 g carb (3 g dietary fibre, 6 g sugar), 75 mg chol, 569 mg sodium, 708 mg potassium. % RDI: 6% calcium, 24% iron, 13% vit A, 95% vit C, 15% folate.

1 tsp	vegetable oil
900 g	boneless skinless chicken thighs, cut in ¾-inch pieces
2 cups	sliced leeks (white and light green parts only)
6	cloves garlic, thinly sliced
1	300 ml jar roasted red peppers, drained and chopped
1 tbsp	tomato paste
¼ tsp	salt
1	796 ml can stewed whole tomatoes
675 g	mini yellow-fleshed potatoes, scrubbed and halved
1 cup	frozen peas, thawed
2 tbsp	chopped fresh parsley

The Ultimate Chicken & Dumplings

MAKES 8 SERVINGS
HANDS-ON TIME 1¼ HOURS
TOTAL TIME 1½ HOURS

CHICKEN STEW

6	strips bacon, chopped
2 tsp	olive oil
1	227 g pkg cremini mushrooms, quartered
900 g	boneless skinless chicken thighs
2 tbsp	water
2	onions, chopped
3	carrots, chopped
3	ribs celery, chopped
3	cloves garlic, minced
½ cup	all-purpose flour
4 cups	sodium-reduced chicken broth
1 cup	dry white wine
500 g	yellow-fleshed potatoes, peeled and cubed
1	bay leaf
½ tsp	each pepper, dried marjoram and dried savory
¼ tsp	salt
1 cup	frozen peas
⅔ cup	35% cream
½ cup	frozen corn
¼ cup	chopped fresh parsley

DUMPLINGS

1½ cups	all-purpose flour
2 tbsp	each chopped fresh parsley and fresh chives
1 tsp	each baking powder and chopped fresh thyme
¼ tsp	each salt and baking soda
2 tbsp	cold butter, cubed
⅔ cup	buttermilk

CHICKEN STEW In Dutch oven or large heavy-bottomed pot, cook bacon over medium heat, stirring occasionally, until crisp, about 6 minutes. Using slotted spoon, transfer bacon to medium bowl. Set aside.

Transfer 3 tbsp fat from pot to small bowl (add olive oil if needed to make 3 tbsp) and set aside. Discard any remaining fat.

In same pot, heat oil over medium heat; cook mushrooms, stirring occasionally, until softened, about 7 minutes. Add to bowl with bacon.

In same pot, heat half of the reserved fat over medium heat; working in batches, cook chicken, turning once, until browned, about 3 minutes per side. Transfer chicken to separate bowl. Add water to pot, stirring and scraping up any browned bits. Scrape into bowl with chicken. Set aside.

In same pot, heat remaining reserved fat over medium heat; cook onions, carrots and celery, stirring occasionally, until onions are softened, about 10 minutes. Add garlic; cook, stirring, until fragrant, about 1 minute. Sprinkle in flour; cook, stirring often, until light golden, about 2 minutes. Stir in broth and wine until smooth. Add potatoes, bay leaf, pepper, marjoram, savory and salt.

Return chicken and accumulated juices to pot; bring to boil. Reduce heat to medium-low. Simmer, stirring occasionally, until potatoes are fork-tender, about 20 minutes.

Discard bay leaf. Transfer chicken to cutting board. Using 2 forks, shred chicken into bite-size pieces. Return to pot. Stir in mushroom mixture, peas, cream, corn and parsley; bring to simmer.

DUMPLINGS While stew is simmering, in large bowl, whisk together flour, parsley, chives, baking powder, thyme, salt and baking soda. Using pastry blender or 2 knives, cut in butter until mixture resembles fine crumbs with a few larger pieces. Stir in buttermilk to form sticky dough.

On large sheet of parchment paper, shape dough into 7-inch long log; cut crosswise into 8 rounds, reshaping if necessary. Add to stew; cook, covered and without lifting lid, until dumplings are no longer doughy underneath, about 15 minutes.

NUTRITIONAL INFORMATION PER SERVING about 568 cal, 34 g pro, 25 g total fat (11 g sat. fat), 50 g carb (6 g dietary fibre, 8 g sugar), 138 mg chol, 874 mg sodium, 1,000 mg potassium. % RDI: 12% calcium, 29% iron, 83% vit A, 30% vit C, 44% folate.

Classic Bouillabaisse

MAKES 6 SERVINGS
HANDS-ON TIME 30 MINUTES
TOTAL TIME 1¼ HOURS

SEAFOOD STOCK Reserving shells, peel shrimp; cover and refrigerate shrimp for bouillabaisse. In food processor, chop shrimp shells. In Dutch oven or large heavy-bottomed pot, heat oil over medium-high heat; cook shells and leek, stirring, until shells are pink, about 2 minutes.

Add water, clam juice and bay leaves; bring to boil. Reduce heat, cover and simmer for 25 minutes, skimming off any scum. Strain through cheesecloth-lined sieve into large bowl, pressing shells with wooden spoon. *(Make-ahead: Let cool for 30 minutes; refrigerate in airtight container for up to 24 hours.)*

HERBED ROUILLE In small bowl, drizzle wine over bread; let stand for 5 minutes. In food processor, purée together bread, tarragon, oil, hot red pepper, mayonnaise, garlic and ¼ cup of the seafood stock until smooth. Set aside.

BOUILLABAISSE Meanwhile, in Dutch oven or large heavy-bottomed pot, heat oil over medium heat; cook garlic, stirring, until fragrant, about 1 minute. Add fennel and leek; cook, stirring, until fennel is slightly softened, about 5 minutes.

Stir in orange zest and tomato paste; cook over medium-high heat until paste is fragrant, about 1 minute. Add wine; cook for 1 minute. Add strained tomatoes, saffron, salt, pepper and remaining seafood stock; bring to boil. Reduce heat, cover and simmer until fennel is softened, about 30 minutes.

Meanwhile, scrub clams; discard any that do not close when tapped. Add to tomato mixture; cook, covered, over medium-high heat for 3 minutes. Add scallops; cook until tender but firm and clams are opened, about 3 minutes. Discard any clams that do not open. Using slotted spoon, divide seafood among bowls.

Cut fish fillets into 1½-inch chunks. Add fish and reserved shrimp to tomato mixture; cook until shrimp are pink and fish flakes easily when tested, about 2 minutes. Using slotted spoon, divide seafood among bowls. Pour broth over top. Top evenly with rouille. Sprinkle with parsley.

NUTRITIONAL INFORMATION PER SERVING about 338 cal, 38 g pro, 14 g total fat (2 g sat. fat), 12 g carb (2 g dietary fibre, 3 g sugar), 139 mg chol, 583 mg sodium, 1,008 mg potassium. % RDI: 12% calcium, 46% iron, 13% vit A, 32% vit C, 19% folate.

SEAFOOD STOCK

450 g	unpeeled jumbo shrimp (21 to 25 count)
1 tsp	olive oil
1	leek, sliced
6 cups	water
2	236 ml bottles clam juice
2	bay leaves

HERBED ROUILLE

3 tbsp	dry white wine
1 cup	chopped baguette
3 tbsp	chopped fresh tarragon
3 tbsp	olive oil
half	hot red pepper, seeded
1 tbsp	light mayonnaise
1	clove garlic

BOUILLABAISSE

1 tbsp	olive oil
2	cloves garlic, minced
half	bulb fennel, trimmed, cored and thinly sliced
1	leek (white and light green parts only), sliced
1 tbsp	grated orange zest
1 tbsp	tomato paste
1 cup	dry white wine
½ cup	bottled strained tomatoes (passata)
½ tsp	saffron threads
¼ tsp	each salt and pepper
12	littleneck clams (about 790 g total)
6	large scallops (about 255 g total)
450 g	assorted boneless skinless fish fillets (such as cod or halibut)
¼ cup	chopped fresh parsley

MAKES 4 SERVINGS
HANDS-ON TIME 20 MINUTES
TOTAL TIME 30 MINUTES

Cod & Chickpea Stew

3 tbsp	extra-virgin olive oil, divided
1	onion, thinly sliced
half	bulb fennel, thinly sliced and fronds reserved
3	cloves garlic, thinly sliced
½ tsp	crushed fennel seeds (optional)
¼ tsp	salt
1	796 ml can plum tomatoes, chopped
1	540 ml can chickpeas, drained and rinsed
1	236 ml bottle clam juice
450 g	cod, cut in 1-inch pieces
pinch	pepper
	crusty baguette (optional)

In large pot, heat 2 tbsp of the oil over medium heat; cook onion, fennel, garlic, fennel seeds (if using) and salt, stirring occasionally, until softened, about 5 minutes.

Stir in tomatoes, chickpeas, clam juice and 1 cup water; bring to boil. Reduce heat to medium; cook until slightly thickened, about 10 minutes.

Add fish; cook for 2 to 3 minutes.

Divide among bowls. Drizzle with remaining 1 tbsp oil; sprinkle with pepper and reserved fennel fronds. Serve with baguette (if using).

NUTRITIONAL INFORMATION PER SERVING about 412 cal, 31 g pro, 13 g total fat (2 g sat. fat), 44 g carb (8 g dietary fibre, 12 g sugar), 48 mg chol, 651 mg sodium, 1,416 mg potassium. % RDI: 15% calcium, 41% iron, 14% vit A, 75% vit C, 95% folate.

Thai Peanut, Grapefruit & Chicken Salad

MAKES 4 SERVINGS
HANDS-ON TIME 30 MINUTES
TOTAL TIME 30 MINUTES

PEANUT GRAPEFRUIT DRESSING Slice top and bottom off each grapefruit; cut down sides to remove peel and pith. Working over small bowl, cut between membranes to release sections. Squeeze membranes to release remaining juice. Remove segments from juice; set both aside. *(Make-ahead: Cover and refrigerate for up to 24 hours.)*

In small bowl, whisk together ¼ cup of the grapefruit juice, the peanut butter, oil, mint, honey, garlic, fish sauce and soy sauce. Add more grapefruit juice, 1 tbsp at a time, if necessary, until desired consistency.

CHICKEN SALAD Remove and discard skin from chicken. Remove meat from bones and shred; place in large bowl. Add kale; drizzle with dressing, tossing to coat. Arrange on platter; garnish with grapefruit segments, peanuts and mint.

NUTRITIONAL INFORMATION PER SERVING about 539 cal, 44 g pro, 31 g total fat (5 g sat. fat), 29 g carb (7 g dietary fibre, 15 g sugar), 152 mg chol, 673 mg sodium, 1,201 mg potassium. % RDI: 19% calcium, 25% iron, 105% vit A, 272% vit C, 93% folate.

PEANUT GRAPEFRUIT DRESSING

2	grapefruit
2 tbsp	smooth peanut butter, preferably natural
2 tbsp	vegetable oil
2 tbsp	chopped fresh mint
1 tbsp	liquid honey
2	cloves garlic, finely grated or pressed
1 tsp	fish sauce
1 tsp	soy sauce

CHICKEN SALAD

1	deli rotisserie chicken (about 900 g)
6 cups	baby kale
½ cup	chopped peanuts, toasted
6 to 8	whole mint leaves, torn

TEST KITCHEN TIP

On busy weeknights, a deli rotisserie chicken is an easy way to add protein to dinner salads or pasta dishes.

Moroccan Chicken Couscous Salad

MAKES 4 TO 6 SERVINGS
HANDS-ON TIME 10 MINUTES
TOTAL TIME 30 MINUTES

CHICKEN COUSCOUS SALAD

1 cup	boiling water
1 cup	whole wheat couscous
2 cups	diced cooked chicken
1 cup	grape tomatoes, halved lengthwise
1	sweet red pepper, diced
half	English cucumber, chopped
⅓ cup	salted dry-roasted almonds, coarsely chopped
2	green onions, thinly sliced
2 tbsp	chopped fresh cilantro
2 tbsp	chopped fresh mint

MOROCCAN DRESSING

¼ cup	olive oil
¼ cup	lemon juice
1 tbsp	liquid honey
½ tsp	each salt and ground cumin
¼ tsp	each cinnamon and chili powder
¼ tsp	each black pepper and cayenne pepper

CHICKEN COUSCOUS SALAD In large heatproof bowl, stir boiling water with couscous; cover and let stand until absorbed, about 5 minutes. Fluff with fork; let cool to room temperature.

Add chicken, tomatoes, orange and red peppers, cucumber, almonds, green onions, cilantro and mint.

MOROCCAN DRESSING Whisk together oil, lemon juice, honey, cumin, salt, cinnamon, chili powder, black pepper and cayenne pepper. Drizzle over salad and toss gently.

NUTRITIONAL INFORMATION PER EACH OF 6 SERVINGS about 362 cal, 21 g pro, 17 g total fat (3 g sat. fat), 34 g carb (6 g dietary fibre), 42 mg chol, 265 mg sodium, 362 mg potassium. % RDI: 5% calcium, 19% iron, 10% vit A, 75% vit C, 10% folate.

Crispy Tortilla Ancho Chicken Salad

MAKES 4 SERVINGS
HANDS-ON TIME 15 MINUTES
TOTAL TIME 15 MINUTES

ANCHO CHICKEN SALAD Toss tortilla strips with 1 tsp of the oil. Heat large nonstick skillet over medium-high heat; cook strips, tossing often, until golden, about 2 minutes. Transfer to bowl.

Add remaining 2 tsp oil to pan; cook chicken, sweet pepper, garlic, chili powder, pepper and salt, stirring often, until chicken is no longer pink inside, about 4 minutes.

Stir in beans, corn, green onions and lime juice; cook until warmed through, about 3 minutes.

HONEY LIME DRESSING In large bowl, whisk together oil, lime juice, honey and salt. Add lettuce and toss. Spoon chicken mixture over top; sprinkle with cheddar, avocado and tortilla strips.

NUTRITIONAL INFORMATION PER SERVING about 539 cal, 36 g pro, 29 g total fat (6 g sat. fat), 35 g carb (9 g dietary fibre, 6 g sugar), 81 mg chol, 496 mg sodium, 958 mg potassium. % RDI: 14% calcium, 22% iron, 36% vit A, 63% vit C, 56% folate.

ANCHO CHICKEN SALAD

3	small flour tortillas, halved and cut crosswise in ½-inch wide strips
1 tbsp	vegetable oil, divided
450 g	boneless skinless chicken breasts, cut in ¾-inch cubes
1	sweet pepper, chopped
2	cloves garlic, minced
1¼ tsp	ancho chili powder
¼ tsp	pepper
pinch	salt
1 cup	rinsed drained canned black beans
½ cup	frozen corn kernels
2	green onions, chopped
1 tbsp	lime juice
4 cups	torn leaf lettuce
½ cup	shredded old cheddar cheese
1	avocado, pitted, peeled and chopped

HONEY LIME DRESSING

3 tbsp	extra-virgin olive oil
2 tbsp	lime juice
2 tsp	liquid honey
pinch	salt

TEST KITCHEN TIP

Toasted tortilla strips also make a great topping for soups and chilies; add them just before serving to keep their crunch.

MAKES 4 SERVINGS
HANDS-ON TIME 15 MINUTES
TOTAL TIME 15 MINUTES

Chicken Waldorf Wedge Salad

1	clove garlic, minced
1 cup	Balkan-style yogurt
⅓ cup	chopped parsley (approx)
⅓ cup	extra-virgin olive oil, divided
8 tsp	lemon juice, divided
½ tsp	salt
2	ribs celery, trimmed, leaves reserved and ribs chopped
1	peach, cut in 1-inch chunks
2 cups	chopped cooked boneless skinless chicken breast (about 1 large breast)
1½ cups	red grapes, halved
4	rounds (each 1 inch thick) iceberg lettuce (about 1 head)
1 cup	walnuts, toasted and chopped
½ cup	crumbled blue cheese or feta cheese

In small bowl, stir together garlic, yogurt, parsley, ¼ cup of the oil, 2 tbsp of the lemon juice and the salt.

In large bowl, toss together chopped celery, peach, chicken, grapes and remaining oil and lemon juice to coat.

Place 1 lettuce round on each of 4 plates; drizzle with dressing. Top with chicken mixture; sprinkle with walnuts, blue cheese, celery leaves and more parsley, if desired.

NUTRITIONAL INFORMATION PER SERVING about 685 cal, 34 g pro, 51 g total fat (11 g sat. fat), 28 g carb (6 g dietary fibre, 20 g sugar), 87 mg chol, 706 mg sodium, 1,054 mg potassium. % RDI: 25% calcium, 25% iron, 20% vit A, 45% vit C, 75% folate.

TEST KITCHEN TIP

We swapped the classic wedge shape for a round, which makes for easy presentation. If you prefer wedges, quarter an iceberg head, cutting through the core so each quarter holds together.

Ginger Miso Steak Salad

MAKES 4 SERVINGS
HANDS-ON TIME 15 MINUTES
TOTAL TIME 20 MINUTES

Rub steak all over with salt and pepper. In cast-iron or heavy-bottomed skillet, heat vegetable oil and butter over medium-high heat; cook steak, turning once, until desired doneness, 8 to 10 minutes for medium-rare. Transfer to cutting board; let rest for 5 minutes. Thinly slice across the grain.

While steak is resting, in bowl, whisk together cilantro, vinegar, miso paste, ginger, olive oil, garlic, chili garlic paste and 3 tbsp water.

In large bowl, toss together lettuce, yellow pepper, cucumber and half of the dressing. Divide lettuce mixture and steak among 4 plates; drizzle with remaining dressing.

NUTRITIONAL INFORMATION PER SERVING about 303 cal, 28 g pro, 17 g total fat (6 g sat. fat), 9 g carb (2 g dietary fibre, 3 g sugar), 50 mg chol, 561 mg sodium, 732 mg potassium. % RDI: 5% calcium, 26% iron, 31% vit A, 100% vit C, 35% folate.

450 g	beef flank marinating steak
¼ tsp	each salt and pepper
2 tsp	vegetable oil
2 tsp	butter
2 tbsp	chopped fresh cilantro
2 tbsp	unseasoned rice vinegar
2 tbsp	white miso paste
1 tbsp	grated fresh ginger
1 tbsp	olive oil
1	clove garlic, minced
½ tsp	chili garlic paste
2	heads Boston lettuce, torn
1	sweet yellow or red pepper, thinly sliced
half	English cucumber, halved lengthwise and sliced crosswise

MAKES 4 SERVINGS
HANDS-ON TIME 20 MINUTES
TOTAL TIME 20 MINUTES

Easy Niçoise Salad

1	400 g pkg haricots verts, trimmed
3	anchovy fillets, minced
1	shallot, finely chopped
⅓ cup	extra-virgin olive oil
2 tbsp	chopped tarragon
2 tbsp	white wine vinegar
1 tsp	Dijon mustard
6 cups	baby kale or baby arugula
2 cups	cherry tomatoes, halved
4	peeled hard-cooked eggs, quartered
3	142 g cans water-packed chunk light tuna, drained
¼ cup	pitted black olives (such as Niçoise or Kalamata), chopped
2 tbsp	rinsed drained capers

In large heatproof bowl, cover haricots verts with boiling water; cover and let stand until tender, about 10 minutes. Drain; transfer to bowl of ice water to chill. Drain; pat dry.

Meanwhile, in large bowl, stir together anchovies, shallot, oil, tarragon, vinegar and mustard. Reserve ¼ cup in small bowl. Add haricots verts, kale and tomatoes to remaining vinaigrette; toss to coat.

Divide salad among serving plates; top with eggs, fish, olives and capers; drizzle with reserved ¼ cup vinaigrette.

NUTRITIONAL INFORMATION PER SERVING about 439 cal, 29 g pro, 31 g total fat (6 g sat. fat), 11 g carb (3 g dietary fibre, 4 g sugar), 245 mg chol, 644 mg sodium, 444 mg potassium. % RDI: 10% calcium, 18% iron, 29% vit A, 32% vit C, 39% folate.

TEST KITCHEN TIP

Haricots verts, or French green beans, are younger and thinner than other green beans. You can substitute with thicker varieties; simply halve them and extend the standing time to about 15 minutes.

Spicy Salmon Poke Bowls

MAKES 4 SERVINGS
HANDS-ON TIME 20 MINUTES
TOTAL TIME 45 MINUTES

SRIRACHA VINAIGRETTE In small bowl, whisk together vinegar, sriracha, honey, sesame oil and salt; gradually whisk in canola oil in thin steady stream.

POKE BOWLS In bowl, toss fish with ¼ cup of the Sriracha Vinaigrette; cover and refrigerate for 30 minutes.

Meanwhile, in saucepan, bring water and farro to boil over high heat; reduce heat to medium-low, cover and simmer for 30 minutes. Drain.

Divide farro, fish, arugula, cucumbers, radishes (if using) and avocado among serving bowls; drizzle each with 4½ tsp of the remaining Sriracha Vinaigrette. Sprinkle with green onions, sesame seeds and seaweed salad (if using).

NUTRITIONAL INFORMATION PER SERVING about 756 cal, 34 g pro, 41 g total fat (6 g sat. fat), 61 g carb (8 g dietary fibre, 5 g sugar), 57 mg chol, 472 mg sodium, 721 mg potassium. % RDI: 11% calcium, 18% iron, 8% vit A, 22% vit C, 39% folate.

SRIRACHA VINAIGRETTE

⅓ **cup**	white vinegar or rice vinegar
4½ **tsp**	sriracha
2 **tsp**	liquid honey
¾ **tsp**	sesame oil
½ **tsp**	salt
⅓ **cup**	canola oil

POKE BOWLS

450 g	skinless salmon fillet, diced
4½ cups	water
1½ cups	farro, rinsed
6 cups	arugula
2	mini cucumbers, thinly sliced
8	radishes, thinly sliced (optional)
1	avocado, thinly sliced
2	green onions, thinly sliced
2 tbsp	black sesame seeds, toasted seaweed salad (optional)

TEST KITCHEN TIP

Try a spoonful or two of Japanese-style wakame (seaweed) salad on top of this bowl. Seaweed salad is often sold in small containers in Asian grocery stores or in the salad section of large supermarkets.

MAKES 4 SERVINGS
HANDS-ON TIME 25 MINUTES
TOTAL TIME 30 MINUTES

Orange Salmon & Orzo Salad

ORANGE-CHIVE DRESSING

½ tsp	grated orange zest
3 tbsp	orange juice
2 tbsp	chopped fresh chives
2 tsp	Dijon mustard
1 tsp	liquid honey
1	clove garlic, finely grated or pressed
½ tsp	each salt and pepper
⅓ cup	vegetable oil

ORZO SALAD

450 g	skinless salmon fillet
pinch	each salt and pepper
¼ cup	chopped fresh parsley
4 tsp	Dijon mustard
2 tsp	grated orange zest
1½ cups	orzo
2 cups	snow peas, trimmed and sliced diagonally
8 cups	baby arugula
2 cups	watercress leaves or living cress leaves

ORANGE-CHIVE DRESSING In small bowl, whisk together orange zest, orange juice, chives, mustard, honey, garlic, salt and pepper. Slowly whisk in oil. Set aside.

ORZO SALAD Preheat oven to 400°F. Sprinkle fish with salt and pepper. Stir together parsley, mustard and orange zest; spread over fish. Place on lightly greased foil-lined baking sheet. Bake until fish flakes easily when tested, about 15 minutes. Transfer to cutting board; chop or break apart into large chunks.

While fish is baking, in large pot of boiling salted water, cook pasta until almost al dente, about 8 minutes. Add snow peas and cook until pasta is al dente and peas are bright green and tender-crisp, about 30 seconds. Drain.

In large bowl, toss together pasta mixture, arugula, watercress and dressing. Gently fold in fish.

NUTRITIONAL INFORMATION PER SERVING about 635 cal, 32 g pro, 31 g total fat (4 g sat. fat), 56 g carb (4 g dietary fibre, 6 g sugar), 55 mg chol, 714 mg sodium, 721 mg potassium. % RDI: 11% calcium, 21% iron, 20% vit A, 75% vit C, 43% folate.

Kale Buttermilk Caesar Salad
With Smoked Trout

MAKES 4 SERVINGS
HANDS-ON TIME 15 MINUTES
TOTAL TIME 15 MINUTES

BUTTERMILK CAESAR DRESSING In small bowl, whisk together anchovies (if using), buttermilk, yogurt, oil, lemon zest, lemon juice, salt and pepper; stir in Parmesan.

KALE SALAD In large bowl, using hands, rub kale with oil until kale is softened, about 1 minute. Add broccoli and chickpeas. Drizzle with Buttermilk Caesar Dressing; toss to coat. Divide among serving plates; top with fish. Sprinkle with almonds, and with roasted chickpeas and Parmesan (if using).

NUTRITIONAL INFORMATION PER SERVING about 432 cal, 28 g pro, 25 g total fat (5 g sat. fat), 29 g carb (9 g dietary fibre, 7 g sugar), 39 mg chol, 982 mg sodium, 590 mg potassium. % RDI: 25% calcium, 20% iron, 48% vit A, 147% vit C, 52% folate.

BUTTERMILK CAESAR DRESSING

2	anchovy fillets (optional), finely chopped
⅓ cup	buttermilk
⅓ cup	Balkan-style yogurt
2 tbsp	extra-virgin olive oil
2 tsp	lemon zest
2 tbsp	lemon juice
¼ tsp	each salt and pepper
⅔ cup	finely grated Parmesan cheese

KALE SALAD

8 cups	torn stemmed kale (about 1 bunch)
1 tsp	extra-virgin olive oil
4 cups	sliced broccoli florets
1	540 ml can chickpeas, drained and rinsed
2	100 g pkgs smoked trout or salmon, cut in bite-size pieces
½ cup	unsalted roasted almonds, chopped
	roasted chickpeas and/or finely grated Parmesan cheese (optional)

TEST KITCHEN TIP

Raw kale is nutritious and adds tasty crunch to salads, but its robust texture can seem a little tough. Massaging kale leaves with oil will soften them.

Chipotle Steak & Avocado Bowls

MAKES 4 SERVINGS
HANDS-ON TIME 30 MINUTES
TOTAL TIME 45 MINUTES

1 cup	red jasmine rice

GREEN ONION VINAIGRETTE

2 cups	baby spinach
⅓ cup	canola oil
¼ cup	cider vinegar
2	small cloves garlic, minced
1	green onion, chopped
2 tsp	liquid honey
½ tsp	salt

CHIPOTLE STEAK

450 g	top sirloin grilling steak (¾ inch thick)
2 tsp	canola oil
¾ tsp	salt
¾ tsp	chipotle chili powder

TOPPINGS

2	corncobs, husked
2	jalapeño peppers, sliced
6 cups	baby spinach
1	avocado, diced
⅓ cup	pepitas, toasted
2	green onions, thinly sliced
½ cup	crumbled feta cheese
	lime wedges and/or sour cream (optional)

Cook rice according to package directions; fluff with fork.

GREEN ONION VINAIGRETTE Meanwhile, in 2-cup liquid measure or small bowl, combine spinach, oil, vinegar, garlic, green onion, honey and salt; using immersion blender, purée until smooth. Set aside.

CHIPOTLE STEAK Rub steak with oil; sprinkle with salt and chili powder. In cast-iron skillet, cook steak over medium heat, flipping once, until desired doneness, 6 to 8 minutes for medium-rare. Transfer to cutting board; tent with foil. Let rest for 10 minutes before slicing across the grain.

TOPPINGS Meanwhile, wipe pan clean. Cut kernels from corncobs; cook corn and jalapeño peppers in even layer over medium-high heat, without stirring, 1 to 2 minutes. Stir; continue to cook until charred, 1 to 2 minutes.

Divide rice, steak, corn mixture, spinach, avocado, pepitas and green onions among serving bowls; drizzle each with ¼ cup of the Green Onion Vinaigrette. Sprinkle with feta; serve with lime wedges and sour cream (if using).

NUTRITIONAL INFORMATION PER SERVING about 692 cal, 33 g pro, 38 g total fat (5 g sat. fat), 59 g carb (8 g dietary fibre, 6 sugar), 53 mg chol, 801 mg sodium, 926 mg potassium. % RDI: 5% calcium, 46% iron, 35% vit A, 42% vit C, 62% folate.

TEST KITCHEN TIP

Charring the jalapeños adds a smoky flavour and mellows their spiciness. For a milder dish, remove their seeds and white veins. That's where capsaicin, the natural chemical that makes peppers hot, is concentrated.

Chicken Shawarma Bowls

MAKES 4 SERVINGS
HANDS-ON TIME 30 MINUTES
TOTAL TIME 30 MINUTES

Cook bulgur according to package directions; fluff with fork.

Meanwhile, in bowl, whisk together warm water, tahini, lemon zest, lemon juice, 1 tbsp of the oil, the garlic and ¾ tsp of the salt; set aside.

Sprinkle chicken with pepper and remaining ½ tsp salt. In large nonstick skillet, heat remaining 1 tbsp oil over medium-high heat; cook chicken, flipping once, until golden and juices run clear when thickest part is pierced, 8 to 10 minutes. Transfer to cutting board and slice.

Divide bulgur, chicken, baby greens, red onion, tomatoes and parsley among serving bowls; drizzle each with one quarter of the dressing. Top with turnips, pistachios and hot pepper sauce (if using).

NUTRITIONAL INFORMATION PER SERVING about 452 cal, 27 g pro, 23 g total fat (4 g sat. fat), 39 g carb (8 g dietary fibre, 4 g sugar), 67 mg chol, 824 mg sodium, 746 mg potassium. % RDI: 14% calcium, 35% iron, 44% vit A, 53% vit C, 43% folate.

1 cup	medium bulgur
½ cup	warm water
⅓ cup	tahini
1 tsp	lemon zest
¼ cup	lemon juice
2 tbsp	extra-virgin olive oil, divided
2	cloves garlic, minced
1¼ tsp	salt, divided
400 g	boneless skinless chicken thighs
½ tsp	pepper
8 cups	mixed baby greens
½ cup	thinly sliced red onion
8	cocktail tomatoes, cut in wedges
1 cup	parsley, chopped
	pickled turnips, chopped pistachios and/or hot pepper sauce (optional)

MAKES 4 SERVINGS
HANDS-ON TIME 15 MINUTES
TOTAL TIME 30 MINUTES

Peanut Shrimp Crunch Bowls

1 cup	red quinoa, rinsed

SPICY PEANUT DRESSING

⅓ cup	natural peanut butter
⅓ cup	water
3 tbsp	white vinegar
4 tsp	sodium-reduced soy sauce
4 tsp	Asian chili paste (such as sambal oelek)
¼ tsp	each salt and pepper

TOPPINGS

2 tsp	canola oil
400 g	large shrimp (31 to 40 count), peeled and deveined
¼ tsp	each salt and pepper
8 cups	baby kale
2 cups	snow peas, trimmed and halved diagonally
1	carrot, julienned
⅓ cup	sliced red onion
½ cup	cilantro sprigs
⅓ cup	unsalted roasted peanuts, chopped
1	red Thai bird's-eye pepper, sliced (optional)
4	lime wedges

In saucepan, cook quinoa according to package directions; fluff with fork.

SPICY PEANUT DRESSING Meanwhile, in bowl, whisk together peanut butter, water, vinegar, soy sauce, chili paste, salt and pepper; set aside.

TOPPINGS In large nonstick skillet, heat oil over high heat; working in batches, cook shrimp, salt and pepper, stirring, until shrimp are pink and opaque throughout, 2 to 3 minutes.

Stir ⅓ cup of the Spicy Peanut Dressing into quinoa. Divide quinoa, shrimp, kale, snow peas, carrot and red onion among serving bowls; drizzle each with 2 tbsp of the remaining Spicy Peanut Dressing. Sprinkle with cilantro, peanuts and Thai pepper (if using); serve with lime wedges.

NUTRITIONAL INFORMATION PER SERVING about 542 cal, 34 g pro, 26 g total fat (3 g sat. fat), 49 g carb (10 g dietary fibre, 8 g sugar), 114 mg chol, 737 mg sodium, 1,088 mg potassium. % RDI: 16% calcium, 44% iron, 116% vit A, 125% vit C, 87% folate.

TEST KITCHEN TIP

If you don't have Asian chili paste on hand, use sriracha or another hot sauce to taste.

Korean-Style Rice Bowls

MAKES 4 SERVINGS
HANDS-ON TIME 30 MINUTES
TOTAL TIME 30 MINUTES

In saucepan, cook rice according to package directions. Fluff with fork.

HOT PEPPER DRESSING Meanwhile in bowl, whisk together oil, vinegar, hot pepper paste, sugar and salt.

TOPPINGS In large nonstick skillet, heat 1 tbsp of the sesame oil over medium-high heat; cook beef, white parts of green onions and garlic until browned, breaking up beef with wooden spoon, about 5 minutes. Stir in hot pepper paste, soy sauce, sesame seeds and sugar. Cook until slightly thickened, about 2 minutes; transfer to bowl.

In same pan over medium heat, cook spinach and 1 tbsp water until wilted, 1 to 2 minutes. Transfer to separate bowl.

Wipe pan clean; return to medium heat. Add remaining 1 tsp sesame oil. Crack eggs into pan; cook until whites are set but yolks are still runny, 2 to 3 minutes.

Divide rice among bowls. Top with beef mixture, spinach, beets, zucchini and green parts of green onions. Top each with 1 egg. Drizzle with dressing; sprinkle with more sesame seeds, if desired. Stir together ingredients before eating.

NUTRITIONAL INFORMATION PER SERVING about 725 cal, 35 g pro, 39 g total fat (10 g sat. fat), 58 g carb (4 g dietary fibre, 13 g sugar), 250 mg chol, 1,000 mg sodium, 1,461 mg potassium. % RDI: 11% calcium, 37% iron, 8% vit A, 39% vit C, 86% folate.

1 cup	long-grain white rice, rinsed

HOT PEPPER DRESSING

¼ cup	canola oil
3 tbsp	rice vinegar
1 tbsp	Korean hot pepper paste (gochujang) or 2 tsp sriracha
1 tsp	granulated sugar
¼ tsp	salt

TOPPINGS

4 tsp	sesame oil, divided
450 g	lean ground beef
4	green onions, thinly sliced (white and green parts separated)
4	cloves garlic, minced
2 tbsp	Korean hot pepper paste (gochujang) or 4 tsp sriracha
2 tbsp	soy sauce
2 tbsp	toasted sesame seeds (approx)
4 tsp	granulated sugar
1	142 g pkg baby spinach
1 tbsp	water
4	eggs
half	340 g pkg spiral-cut beets
half	340 g pkg spiral-cut zucchini

TEST KITCHEN TIP

Look for packaged spiral-cut vegetables in the produce section of the supermarket. You can use matchstick-cut carrots in place of the beets, if you prefer.

MAKES 4 SERVINGS
HANDS-ON TIME 25 MINUTES
TOTAL TIME 25 MINUTES

Pork & Chili Pepper Bowls

1 cup	long-grain white rice, rinsed

TOPPINGS

1	Thai bird's-eye pepper, halved crosswise and divided
450 g	lean ground pork
pinch	salt
2 tbsp	vegetable oil, divided
2 cups	green beans, cut in ½-inch pieces
3	cloves garlic, minced
4 tsp	grated fresh ginger
2 tbsp	water
1 tbsp	unseasoned rice vinegar
1 tsp	fish sauce
½ tsp	packed brown sugar
4	eggs
½ cup	chopped fresh cilantro (optional)
2	green onions, sliced (optional)

In saucepan, cook rice according to package directions. Fluff with fork.

TOPPINGS Mince half of the Thai pepper; thinly slice remaining half. Set aside.

Sprinkle pork with salt. In large nonstick skillet, cook pork and salt over medium-high heat, breaking up with spoon, until no longer pink, about 8 minutes. Scrape into bowl. Set aside.

In same pan, heat 1 tbsp of the oil over medium heat; cook green beans, garlic, ginger and minced Thai pepper, stirring occasionally, until green beans are tender-crisp, about 5 minutes. Add pork, water, vinegar, fish sauce and brown sugar; cook, stirring, until heated through, about 2 minutes. Divide rice among serving bowls; top with pork mixture. Keep warm. Wipe pan clean.

In same pan, heat remaining 1 tbsp oil over medium heat; cook eggs until whites are set but yolks are still runny, about 3 minutes.

Arrange 1 egg over each pork bowl. Sprinkle with cilantro and green onions (if using) and sliced Thai pepper.

NUTRITIONAL INFORMATION PER SERVING about 582 cal, 33 g pro, 30 g total fat (9 g sat. fat), 43 g carb (2 g dietary fibre, 2 g sugar), 266 mg chol, 207 mg sodium, 556 mg potassium. % RDI: 7% calcium, 18% iron, 14% vit A, 12% vit C, 26% folate.

One-Pan Crispy Chicken
With Roasted Veggies

MAKES 4 SERVINGS
HANDS-ON TIME 15 MINUTES
TOTAL TIME 40 MINUTES

Preheat oven to 450°F. In small bowl, stir together parsley, tarragon, garlic, all but 1 tsp of the oil, the lemon juice and cayenne pepper. Set aside.

Sprinkle cauliflower and chicken with all but pinch each of the salt and pepper. Toss cauliflower with half of the parsley mixture; arrange on half of foil-lined baking sheet. Toss chicken with remaining parsley mixture; spread on other half of pan. Bake, turning once, for 20 minutes.

Toss green beans with remaining 1 tsp oil and remaining salt and pepper; add to pan alongside cauliflower, rearranging to fit. Bake until vegetables are tender and juices run clear when thickest part of chicken is pierced, about 6 minutes. Remove vegetables to plate; keep warm. Broil chicken, turning once, until golden, about 4 minutes. Serve with vegetables.

NUTRITIONAL INFORMATION PER SERVING about 415 cal, 30 g pro, 27 g total fat (6 g sat. fat), 14 g carb (6 g dietary fibre, 4 g sugar), 91 mg chol, 399 mg sodium, 621 mg potassium. % RDI: 8% calcium, 21% iron, 13% vit A, 127% vit C, 5% folate.

¼ cup	chopped fresh parsley
1 tbsp	chopped fresh tarragon
3	cloves garlic, minced
3 tbsp	olive oil, divided
2 tsp	lemon juice
pinch	cayenne pepper
4 cups	bite-size cauliflower florets (about half head)
8	bone-in skin-on chicken drumsticks (about 900 g total)
½ tsp	each salt and pepper
450 g	green beans (about 6 cups), trimmed

TEST KITCHEN TIP

Once you turn on the broiler, keep a close eye on the chicken; it can quickly go from perfectly golden to burned if you aren't careful.

Sheet Pan Greek Chicken & Lemon Potatoes

MAKES 4 SERVINGS
HANDS-ON TIME 10 MINUTES
TOTAL TIME 45 MINUTES

8	bone-in skin-on chicken thighs (about 1.1 kg total)
4	yellow-fleshed potatoes, scrubbed and cut in 1-inch thick rounds
3	cloves garlic, smashed
3 tbsp	olive oil
¼ cup	Greek seasoning
½ tsp	each salt and pepper
1	lemon, halved
4 cups	watercress or arugula

Preheat oven to 450°F. Line baking sheet with parchment paper. On pan, toss together chicken, potatoes, garlic and oil to coat; sprinkle with Greek seasoning, salt and pepper. Arrange in single layer with chicken skin side up. Add lemon, cut side up. Roast, rotating pan halfway through, until juices run clear when thickest part of chicken is pierced and potatoes are fork-tender, 35 to 40 minutes.

Add watercress; toss to combine. Return to oven; roast just until watercress is wilted, 1 to 2 minutes. Squeeze lemon over top; discard lemon halves.

NUTRITIONAL INFORMATION PER SERVING about 524 cal, 56 g pro, 18 g total fat (4 g sat. fat), 42 g carb (7 g dietary fibre, 2 g sugar), 203 mg chol, 999 mg sodium, 1,557 mg potassium. % RDI: 11% calcium, 29% iron, 5% vit A, 178% vit C, 30% folate.

TEST KITCHEN TIP

If you substitute arugula for the watercress, there's no need to return the pan to the oven to wilt the arugula. Just toss and serve.

One-Pan Jerk Chicken Dinner

MAKES 4 SERVINGS
HANDS-ON TIME 10 MINUTES
TOTAL TIME 50 MINUTES

Preheat oven to 425°F. In small bowl, whisk together thyme, garlic powder, salt, allspice, coriander, ginger, pepper and cayenne pepper.

In plastic bag, add chicken and 4 tsp of the thyme mixture. Holding bag closed, shake to coat chicken.

In lightly greased large roasting pan, toss together white potato, sweet potato, red pepper, onion and remaining thyme mixture; arrange vegetables in single layer. Add chicken.

Roast until juices run clear when thickest part of chicken is pierced and potatoes are softened, about 40 minutes. Broil until chicken and vegetables are golden, about 3 minutes.

NUTRITIONAL INFORMATION PER SERVING about 388 cal, 28 g pro, 16 g total fat (4 g sat. fat), 34 g carb (5 g dietary fibre, 8 g sugar), 102 mg chol, 559 mg sodium, 888 mg potassium. % RDI: 6% calcium, 26% iron, 133% vit A, 150% vit C, 16% folate.

2 tsp	dried thyme
1 tsp	garlic powder
¾ tsp	salt
½ tsp	each ground allspice, ground coriander and ground ginger
¼ tsp	pepper
pinch	cayenne pepper
8	skin-on chicken drumsticks (about 900 g total)
300 g	white or yellow-fleshed potato (about 1), cut in wedges
300 g	sweet potato (about 1), cut in wedges
1	sweet red pepper, cut in 1-inch thick slices
1	small onion, cut in wedges

SERVE WITH

Pineapple Salad

In large bowl, whisk together 4 tsp vegetable oil, 1½ tsp lime juice, ½ tsp liquid honey and pinch each salt and pepper. Add 6 cups mixed baby greens, 1 cup chopped cored peeled pineapple and ¼ cup thinly sliced red onion; toss to coat.

Sheet Pan Steak & Potatoes

Page 4

450 g	top sirloin grilling steak (¾ inch thick)
1½ tsp	pepper, divided
1 tsp	garlic salt, divided
4	cloves garlic (skins on), smashed
2	yellow-fleshed potatoes, cut in ¾-inch wedges
1	large red onion, cut in 8 wedges
¼ cup	olive oil, divided
2	bunches Broccolini, trimmed and halved lengthwise
½ cup	mayonnaise
2 tbsp	prepared horseradish
2 tbsp	finely chopped chives

Sprinkle steak with ½ tsp each of the pepper and garlic salt; let stand at room temperature. Meanwhile, position racks in upper third (6 inches from top) and lower third of oven; preheat to 450°F.

On baking sheet, toss together garlic, potatoes, red onion, 3 tbsp of the oil, ½ tsp of the pepper and remaining ½ tsp garlic salt; arrange in single layer. Bake in lower third of oven, flipping halfway through, until vegetables are tender and golden, 25 to 30 minutes.

Meanwhile, place steak in centre of separate baking sheet; arrange Broccolini around steak. Drizzle with remaining 1 tbsp oil. Broil, flipping halfway through, until steak is medium-rare, 6 to 8 minutes. Transfer steak to cutting board; let rest for 5 minutes.

While steak is resting, squeeze garlic into small bowl to release from skins; discard skins. Using fork, mash garlic. Add mayonnaise, horseradish, chives and remaining ½ tsp pepper, stirring to combine.

Slice steak across the grain. Divide steak, Broccolini, potatoes and red onion among plates; serve with mayonnaise mixture.

NUTRITIONAL INFORMATION PER SERVING about 660 cal, 30 g pro, 40 g total fat (7 g sat. fat), 46 g carb (6 g dietary fibre, 9 g sugar), 63 mg chol, 558 mg sodium, 1,444 mg potassium. % RDI:11% calcium, 35% iron, 18% vit A, 128% vit C, 46% folate.

Hearty Italian Pot Roast

MAKES 8 TO 10 SERVINGS
HANDS-ON TIME 45 MINUTES
ROASTING TIME 3½ HOURS
TOTAL TIME 4¼ HOURS

Preheat oven to 325°F. In Dutch oven or large heavy-bottomed pot, heat 1 tbsp of the oil over medium-high heat; working in batches, cook beef, turning occasionally, until browned all over, 3 to 5 minutes. Transfer to 16- x 12-inch roasting pan; set aside.

Reduce heat to medium. Add remaining 1 tbsp oil to Dutch oven; cover and cook garlic, bay leaves, red onion, carrots, celery and fennel seeds, stirring occasionally, until softened, about 8 minutes. Increase heat to medium-high; stir in cocoa powder, rosemary and mushrooms. Add wine; cook, scraping up any browned bits, for 5 minutes. Stir in broth and tomatoes (including juices); bring to boil. Carefully transfer tomato mixture to roasting pan.

Cover roasting pan with foil; braise in oven, turning beef twice, until fork-tender, about 3½ hours.

Transfer beef to cutting board. Remove any twine; slice beef across grain, trimming excess fat. Keep warm.

Skim fat from surface of cooking liquid. Strain cooking liquid and vegetables through sieve into large saucepan. Using metal or wooden spoon, press down on vegetables to extract liquid; discard vegetables.

Place pan over medium-high heat; bring to boil. In small bowl, whisk cornstarch with water; whisk into pan. Simmer, stirring often, until thickened, about 3 minutes. Serve with beef.

2 tbsp	olive oil, divided
2	cross rib or blade pot roasts (each 1.5 to 1.7 kg)
6	cloves garlic, smashed
2	bay leaves
1	red onion, quartered
2	carrots, halved crosswise
2	ribs celery, halved crosswise
2 tsp	fennel seeds
1½ tbsp	cocoa powder
5	sprigs fresh rosemary
1	14 g pkg dried wild mushrooms, coarsely torn
1½ cups	red wine
1	900 ml pkg sodium-reduced beef broth
1	can whole plum tomatoes, coarsely crushed
3 tbsp	cornstarch
3 tbsp	water

NUTRITIONAL INFORMATION PER EACH OF 10 SERVINGS about 220 cal, 31 g pro, 8 g total fat (3 g sat. fat), 7 g carb (1 g dietary fibre, 3 g sugar), 67 mg chol, 267 mg sodium, 621 mg potassium. % RDI: 3% calcium, 26% iron, 19% vit A, 12% vit C, 6% folate.

MAKES 10 ENCHILADAS
HANDS-ON TIME 20 MINUTES
TOTAL TIME 40 MINUTES

Pot Roast Enchiladas

2 cups	sauce from Hearty Italian Pot Roast (see recipe, page 85)
1 cup	bottled strained tomatoes (passata)
2 tbsp	minced pickled jalapeño peppers, divided
1 tbsp	chili powder
1 tsp	dried oregano
1 tsp	ground cumin
3½ cups	loosely packed shredded Hearty Italian Pot Roast (see recipe, page 85)
1	540 ml can sodium-reduced black beans, drained and rinsed
half	370 ml jar sliced roasted red peppers, drained and chopped
10	8-inch soft flour tortillas
2 cups	shredded Monterey Jack cheese
1	green onion, sliced
	sour cream (optional)
	sliced avocado (optional)

Preheat oven to 375°F. In small saucepan, stir together pot roast sauce, strained tomatoes, 1 tbsp of the jalapeño peppers, the chili powder, oregano and cumin over medium heat. Cook, stirring often, until bubbly, about 5 minutes.

Spread about ½ cup of the sauce in bottom of 13- x 9-inch baking dish. In large bowl, mix together 1½ cups of the sauce, remaining 1 tbsp jalapeño peppers, Hearty Italian Pot Roast, black beans and red peppers.

Spoon heaping ⅓ cup of the beef mixture onto centre of each tortilla; roll up. Arrange, seam side down, in single layer in baking dish. Pour remaining sauce over top. Sprinkle with Monterey Jack.

Bake until Monterey Jack is melted and bubbly, about 20 minutes. Garnish with green onion. Serve with sour cream and avocado (if using).

NUTRITIONAL INFORMATION PER ENCHILADA about 319 cal, 25 g pro, 12 g total fat (5 g sat. fat), 28 g carb (5 g dietary fibre, 4 g sugar), 50 mg chol, 695 mg sodium, 598 mg potassium. % RDI: 17% calcium, 29% iron, 21% vit A, 45% vit C, 32% folate.

Corned Beef Cabbage Rolls
With Cider Dijon Sauce

MAKES 18 TO 20 ROLLS
HANDS-ON TIME 1 HOUR
TOTAL TIME 1½ HOURS

CIDER DIJON SAUCE Preheat oven to 350°F. In saucepan, heat oil over medium heat; cook onion and apple, stirring occasionally, until softened and light golden, 10 to 12 minutes. Stir in cider, broth, molasses and Dijon mustard; bring to boil over high heat. Reduce heat and simmer, stirring occasionally, for 15 minutes. Let cool slightly. In blender, purée sauce until smooth.

Return sauce to pan; bring to boil. Whisk in grainy mustard, salt and pepper. Whisk cornstarch with water; whisk into sauce. Bring to boil; cook until thickened, 1 to 2 minutes. *(Make-ahead: Let cool for 30 minutes; refrigerate in airtight container for up to 5 days.)*

CABBAGE ROLLS In large saucepan of boiling salted water, cook carrots and potatoes until fork-tender, 15 to 18 minutes; drain well.

In same pan, melt butter over medium heat; cook garlic and red onion, stirring occasionally, until lightly browned, about 3 minutes. Sprinkle in thyme, caraway seeds, salt and pepper. Turn off heat; return carrots and potatoes to pan. Mash until smooth; stir in milk. Fold in corned beef. *(Make-ahead: Let cool for 30 minutes; refrigerate in airtight container for up to 2 days.)*

In saucepan of boiling water, working in batches, cook cabbage leaves until slightly softened; rinse to cool. Using knife, cut triangle from bottom of each cabbage leaf to remove thick white portion. Divide potato filling among leaves. Tuck in sides and roll up.

ASSEMBLY Spoon one-third of the Cider Dijon Sauce over bottom of 13- x 9-inch baking dish. Place cabbage rolls, seam side down, on top of sauce. Spoon 1 cup of the sauce over cabbage rolls. Cover with parchment paper; seal baking dish with foil. Bake until filling is warm and sauce is bubbly, 45 to 55 minutes. Serve with remaining sauce.

NUTRITIONAL INFORMATION PER EACH OF 20 ROLLS about 125 cal, 5 g pro, 5 g total fat (2 g sat. fat), 17 g carb (2 g dietary fibre, 8 g sugar), 19 mg chol, 512 mg sodium, 302 mg potassium. % RDI: 4% calcium, 8% iron, 35% vit A, 7% vit C, 10% folate.

CIDER DIJON SAUCE

2 tbsp	vegetable oil
1	small onion, sliced
1	McIntosh apple, peeled, cored and chopped
2 cups	apple cider
2 cups	chicken broth
3 tbsp	fancy molasses
1 tbsp	each Dijon mustard and grainy mustard
¼ tsp	each salt and pepper
3 tbsp	cornstarch
3 tbsp	water

CABBAGE ROLLS

3	carrots, sliced
2	yellow-fleshed potatoes, peeled and cubed
2 tbsp	butter
3	cloves garlic, minced
1	red onion, diced
2 tbsp	chopped fresh thyme
1 tbsp	caraway seeds
½ tsp	each salt and pepper
¼ cup	milk
325 g	deli corned beef, diced (about 2 cups)
18 to 20	outer leaves of 1 head napa cabbage

Breaded Pork Chops
With Spiced Potatoes & Carrots

MAKES 4 SERVINGS
HANDS-ON TIME 15 MINUTES
TOTAL TIME 45 MINUTES

SPICED POTATOES & CARROTS

400 g	mini yellow-fleshed potatoes, scrubbed and quartered
3	carrots, halved lengthwise and cut crosswise in ¾-inch pieces
1 tbsp	olive oil
1 tsp	cumin seeds
1 tsp	garlic powder
¼ tsp	each salt and pepper
¼ cup	chopped fresh parsley

BREADED PORK CHOPS

¼ cup	dried bread crumbs
¼ cup	finely grated Parmesan cheese
½ tsp	herbes de Provence
2 tsp	olive oil
4	boneless pork loin chops (about 500 g total), patted dry
1 tbsp	Dijon mustard
pinch	each salt and pepper

SPICED POTATOES & CARROTS Preheat oven to 450°F. In bowl, toss together potatoes, carrots, oil, cumin, garlic powder, salt and pepper. Arrange in single layer on parchment paper–lined baking sheet. Bake, stirring once, until tender and golden, about 40 minutes. Toss with parsley just before serving.

BREADED PORK CHOPS While vegetables are roasting, in large shallow bowl, mix together bread crumbs, Parmesan, herbes de Provence and oil. Rub pork all over with mustard; sprinkle with salt and pepper. Dredge in bread crumb mixture, turning and pressing to coat.

Once vegetables have roasted for 30 minutes, push to 1 side of pan; add pork. Bake until instant-read thermometer inserted sideways into centre of pork reads 155°F, 8 to 10 minutes.

NUTRITIONAL INFORMATION PER SERVING about 424 cal, 34 g pro, 19 g total fat (6 g sat. fat), 30 g carb (4 g dietary fibre, 4 g sugar), 71 mg chol, 444 mg sodium, 1,053 mg potassium. % RDI: 12% calcium, 22% iron, 96% vit A, 25% vit C, 23% folate.

TEST KITCHEN TIP

Herbes de Provence is a fragrant blend of dried herbs that's available in many grocery stores, or you can mix your own: Combine 2 tbsp each dried marjoram, dried oregano, dried thyme and dried savory; ½ tsp each dried basil and dried rosemary; and ¼ tsp dried sage. Store in airtight container at room temperature in dark place for up to 3 months. Makes about ½ cup.

Garlicky Parmesan Salmon & Asparagus

MAKES 4 SERVINGS
HANDS-ON TIME 15 MINUTES
TOTAL TIME 25 MINUTES

Preheat oven to 425°F. Line baking sheet with parchment paper. In small bowl, whisk together oil, garlic, lemon zest, lemon juice, ½ tsp of the salt and ¼ tsp of the pepper.

Place fish in centre of prepared pan; sprinkle with remaining ¼ tsp each salt and pepper. Brush with half of the garlic mixture; sprinkle with ¼ cup of the Parmesan. Bake for 5 minutes. Remove from oven; slide fish to one side of pan.

Add asparagus to pan; brush with remaining garlic mixture. Sprinkle with remaining ¼ cup Parmesan. Return to oven; bake until fish flakes easily when tested, 5 to 7 minutes. Sprinkle with chives.

NUTRITIONAL INFORMATION PER SERVING about 463 cal, 39 g pro, 31 g total fat (6 g sat. fat), 6 g carb (2 g dietary fibre, 2 g sugar), 103 mg chol, 640 mg sodium, 850 mg potassium. % RDI: 12% calcium, 12% iron, 14% vit A, 32% vit C, 92% folate.

3 tbsp	olive oil
2	cloves garlic, minced
1 tsp	lemon zest
2 tbsp	lemon juice
¾ tsp	salt, divided
½ tsp	pepper, divided
4	salmon fillets (about 800 g total)
½ cup	finely grated Parmesan cheese, divided
1	bunch asparagus (about 450 g), trimmed
¼ cup	finely chopped chives

TEST KITCHEN TIP

To remove the fibrous base of the asparagus spear, many cooks hold the spear at the top and bottom before snapping off the base, but this usually removes more than needed. Instead, hold the spear in the middle and at the bottom; gently bend until it snaps. Use this spear as a guide to trim the rest of the bunch using a knife.

MAKES 4 SERVINGS
HANDS-ON TIME 15 MINUTES
TOTAL TIME 35 MINUTES

Sheet Pan Provençal Salmon

3	zucchini, cut in 1-inch pieces
3	cloves garlic, sliced
1	red onion, cut in ½-inch thick wedges
3 tbsp	olive oil, divided
1 tsp	salt, divided
¾ tsp	pepper, divided
4	skin-on salmon fillets (about 450 g total)
2 cups	cherry tomatoes
3 tbsp	red wine vinegar
¼ cup	basil leaves, torn

Arrange rack in top third of oven; preheat to 425°F. Line baking sheet with parchment paper. On pan, toss together zucchini, garlic, red onion, 2 tbsp of the oil and ½ tsp each of the salt and pepper. Roast, stirring halfway through, until tender, about 20 minutes.

Remove from oven; push vegetables to edges of pan. Arrange fish, skin side down, and tomatoes in centre; drizzle with remaining 1 tbsp oil. Sprinkle with remaining ½ tsp salt and ¼ tsp pepper. Return to top rack of oven; broil until fish flakes easily when tested and vegetables are beginning to brown, 6 to 8 minutes. Drizzle with vinegar; sprinkle with basil.

NUTRITIONAL INFORMATION PER SERVING about 402 cal, 27 g pro, 26 g total fat (5 g sat. fat), 16 g carb (4 g dietary fibre, 9 g sugar), 62 mg chol, 680 mg sodium, 1,126 mg potassium. % RDI: 7% calcium, 11% iron, 4% vit A, 81% vit C, 42% folate.

TEST KITCHEN TIP

For best results, position the top rack so it's 6 inches away from the oven's coils.

Mini Fish & Vegetable Pies

MAKES 4 SERVINGS
HANDS-ON TIME 20 MINUTES
TOTAL TIME 30 MINUTES

FISH & VEGETABLE FILLING Preheat oven to 425°F. In Dutch oven or large heavy-bottomed pot, melt butter over medium heat; cook leeks, carrot, celery and garlic, stirring occasionally, until beginning to soften, about 5 minutes.

Add flour; cook, stirring, for 1 minute. Whisk in broth and water; cook, whisking, until slightly thickened, about 2 minutes. Whisk in milk. Remove from heat; stir in fish, peas, dill, lemon juice, mustard, salt and pepper.

MASHED POTATO TOPPING Meanwhile, prick potatoes all over with fork. Microwave on high until fork-tender, about 7 minutes. Set aside until cool enough to handle. Peel potatoes; mash with milk, horseradish, salt and pepper.

Divide fish mixture among four 1-cup ramekins. Spoon potato mixture over each, smoothing tops. Arrange ramekins on baking sheet; bake until filling is bubbly, about 10 minutes.

NUTRITIONAL INFORMATION PER SERVING about 257 cal, 19 g pro, 4 g total fat (2 g sat. fat), 38 g carb (4 g dietary fibre, 6 g sugar), 40 mg chol, 392 mg sodium, 1,000 mg potassium. % RDI: 11% calcium, 21% iron, 42% vit A, 47% vit C, 30% folate.

FISH & VEGETABLE FILLING

2 tsp	unsalted butter
2 cups	sliced leeks (white and light green parts only)
½ cup	diced carrot
½ cup	diced celery
3	cloves garlic, minced
2 tbsp	all-purpose flour
¾ cup	sodium-reduced vegetable broth
¼ cup	water
¼ cup	milk
300 g	cod or other firm whitefish fillet, cut in 1-inch chunks
½ cup	frozen peas
2 tbsp	chopped fresh dill
4 tsp	lemon juice
2 tsp	Dijon mustard
¼ tsp	each salt and pepper

MASHED POTATO TOPPING

2	russet potatoes (about 500 g total)
¼ cup	milk
2 tsp	prepared horseradish
pinch	each salt and pepper

TEST KITCHEN TIP

Rinse leeks thoroughly. They're grown in sandy soil and tend to retain dirt and grit.

Tuna Casserole

MAKES 8 SERVINGS
HANDS-ON TIME 35 MINUTES
TOTAL TIME 35 MINUTES

450 g	rigatoni
1	140 g pkg baby kale mix
2 tbsp	unsalted butter
half	onion, diced
2	ribs celery, diced
3	cloves garlic, finely grated or pressed
2 tsp	dried thyme
4 tbsp	all-purpose flour
3¾ cups	2% milk
½ tsp	each salt and pepper
2	160 g cans oil-packed tuna, drained
1	320 g pkg shredded Italian cheese blend (about 3 cups), divided
1 cup	crushed potato chips

Spray 13- x 9-inch baking dish. In large pot of boiling water, cook pasta for 2 to 3 minutes longer than package directions. Reserving ½ cup of the cooking liquid, drain. Return pasta to pot; add kale. Let stand for 2 minutes; toss to combine. Set aside.

Meanwhile, in separate large saucepan, melt butter over medium-high heat. Add onion and celery; cook, stirring frequently, until onion is softened, about 4 minutes. Add garlic and thyme; cook, stirring, for 30 seconds. Sprinkle in flour; stir, scraping bottom of pan, just until combined. Add milk, salt and pepper; cook, stirring constantly and scraping bottom of pan, until sauce is thick enough to coat back of spoon, 7 to 8 minutes.

Preheat broiler to high. Stir reserved cooking liquid, sauce, tuna and 2 cups of the cheese into pasta mixture. Scrape into prepared dish; sprinkle with remaining cheese. Broil until cheese is golden and bubbly, 30 seconds to 1 minute. Top with potato chips.

NUTRITIONAL INFORMATION PER SERVING about 563 cal, 33 g pro, 22 g total fat (11 g sat. fat), 59 g carb (3 g dietary fibre, 8 g sugar), 52 mg chol, 839 mg sodium, 457 mg potassium. % RDI: 50% calcium, 26% iron, 38% vit A, 47% vit C, 78% folate.

TEST KITCHEN TIP

Cooking the pasta for longer than usual will keep the noodles from soaking up the sauce, making for a creamier casserole.

Hearty Turkey Pot Pies

MAKES 4 SERVINGS
HANDS-ON TIME 25 MINUTES
TOTAL TIME 40 MINUTES

Preheat oven to 450°F. In large skillet, heat oil over medium heat; cook grains, onion, carrot, celery and mushrooms, stirring occasionally, until grains are beginning to soften and onion is softened, about 10 minutes. Add garlic and thyme; cook, stirring, until fragrant. Add flour, stirring to coat; cook, stirring, for 30 seconds.

Increase heat to medium-high. Stir in broth; bring to simmer. Cook, stirring often, until thickened, about 8 minutes. Stir in turkey, peas, cream, salt and pepper; bring to simmer. Cook, stirring, for 1 minute. Divide among four 12-oz mini soufflé dishes. Set aside.

On lightly floured work surface, roll out pastry into 10-inch square; cut into 4 equal squares. Place 1 square over each mini soufflé dish; cut 4 steam vents in top of each. Whisk egg with water; lightly brush over pastry.

Arrange mini soufflé dishes on baking sheet; bake until pastry is puffed and golden and filling is bubbly, about 15 minutes. Let stand for 5 minutes before serving.

NUTRITIONAL INFORMATION PER SERVING about 542 cal, 30 g pro, 25 g total fat (13 g sat. fat), 48 g carb (5 g dietary fibre, 6 g sugar), 96 mg chol, 994 mg sodium, 484 mg potassium. % RDI: 6% calcium, 25% iron, 49% vit A, 8% vit C, 17% folate.

1 tsp	olive oil
⅓ cup	quick-cooking whole grain blend (such as PC Blue Menu Brown Rice With Barley and Spelt Blend)
1	onion, finely chopped
1	carrot, finely chopped
1	rib celery, finely chopped
½ cup	chopped cremini mushrooms
1	clove garlic, minced
½ tsp	chopped fresh thyme
¼ cup	all-purpose flour
2 cups	sodium-reduced chicken broth
2 cups	shredded cooked skinless turkey breast
½ cup	frozen green peas
⅓ cup	35% cream
¾ tsp	each salt and pepper
1	sheet (half 450 g pkg) frozen butter puff pastry, thawed
1	egg
1 tsp	water

TEST KITCHEN TIP

Look for a packaged whole grain blend that cooks in 15 minutes or less to ensure the grains become tender while the pies are baking.

Butternut Squash & Smoked Cheddar Pizza

MAKES 4 SERVINGS
HANDS-ON TIME 15 MINUTES
TOTAL TIME 30 MINUTES

4 tsp	olive oil, divided
1	clove garlic, minced
4 cups	lightly packed baby spinach
¼ tsp	each salt and pepper, divided
2 cups	shaved peeled butternut squash (about ⅛ of a squash)
½ tsp	chopped fresh thyme
2 tsp	cornmeal
350 g	prepared pizza dough
1 cup	shredded smoked cheddar cheese

Position rack in bottom of oven; preheat to 500°F. In large skillet, heat 1 tsp of the oil over medium heat; cook garlic, stirring, until fragrant, about 1 minute. Add spinach; cook, stirring, just until wilted, about 2 minutes. Sprinkle with pinch each of the salt and pepper. Remove from heat; let cool slightly.

Toss together squash, thyme, 1 tsp of the oil and the remaining salt and pepper; set aside.

Lightly grease 17- x 11-inch baking sheet; sprinkle with cornmeal. On lightly floured work surface, roll out or press dough into 17- x 11-inch rectangle. Transfer to pan; prick all over with fork. Brush remaining 2 tsp oil over dough; top with spinach mixture, squash mixture and cheddar.

Bake until crust is golden and crisp and cheddar is bubbly, 12 to 14 minutes. Let cool on pan for 3 minutes before slicing.

NUTRITIONAL INFORMATION PER SERVING about 415 cal, 15 g pro, 20 g total fat (8 g sat. fat), 46 g carb (4 g dietary fibre, 5 g sugar), 30 mg chol, 746 mg sodium, 367 mg potassium. % RDI: 32% calcium, 29% iron, 75% vit A, 13% vit C, 59% folate.

TEST KITCHEN TIP

Use a vegetable peeler to cut evenly thin shavings of butternut squash.

Pan-Fried Trout
With Bacon, Kale & Potatoes

MAKES 4 SERVINGS
HANDS-ON TIME 40 MINUTES
TOTAL TIME 40 MINUTES

In cast-iron or heavy-bottomed skillet, cook bacon over medium heat, stirring, until lightly crisp, about 3 minutes. Add potatoes, garlic, 4 sprigs of the thyme and ¼ tsp each of the salt and pepper; cook, stirring occasionally, until potatoes are browned and beginning to soften, 6 to 8 minutes. Add kale; cook, stirring, until potatoes are fork-tender and kale is wilted, about 2 minutes. Remove from heat; discard thyme. Transfer to platter; keep warm. Wipe pan clean.

Sprinkle fish with remaining ¾ tsp salt and ½ tsp pepper. In same pan, heat 1 tbsp of the oil over medium-high heat; add half of the fish, skin side down, 1 tbsp of the butter and 4 sprigs of the remaining thyme; gently press fish down with spatula for 15 seconds to prevent curling. Cook, tilting pan and spooning butter over fish frequently and flipping once, until fish flakes easily when tested, 4 to 5 minutes. Transfer to plate and discard thyme; wipe pan clean. Repeat with remaining oil, fish, butter and thyme, adding caper berries during last minute of cooking (if using). Remove from heat; discard thyme.

Divide potato mixture among serving plates; top with fish. Sprinkle with sumac (if using). Serve with lemon.

NUTRITIONAL INFORMATION PER SERVING about 533 cal, 37 g pro, 35 g total fat (10 g sat. fat), 18 g carb (2 g dietary fibre, 1 g sugar), 125 mg chol, 893 mg sodium, 1,182 mg potassium. % RDI: 9% calcium, 14% iron, 38% vit A, 68% vit C, 22% folate.

4	strips bacon, coarsely chopped
350 g	mixed mini potatoes, cut in ½-inch thick rounds (about 2½ cups)
5	cloves garlic, halved
12	sprigs thyme, divided
1 tsp	salt, divided
¾ tsp	pepper, divided
half	bunch Tuscan kale, chopped (about 4 cups)
4	skin-on trout fillets (each about 180 g)
2 tbsp	canola oil, divided
2 tbsp	unsalted butter, divided
8	caper berries (optional)
½ tsp	sumac (optional)
1	lemon, sliced

TEST KITCHEN TIP

For crisp skin, we cook the trout fillets in batches and flip them just once.

Turkey, Asiago & Spinach Frittata

MAKES 4 SERVINGS
HANDS-ON TIME 20 MINUTES
TOTAL TIME 30 MINUTES

1 tbsp	olive oil
1	onion, chopped
2	cloves garlic, minced
1½ tsp	chopped fresh thyme
4 cups	lightly packed baby spinach
8	eggs, whisked
¼ cup	milk
¼ tsp	each salt and pepper
1 cup	chopped cooked turkey
½ cup	lightly packed grated Asiago cheese, divided

In 10-inch ovenproof skillet, heat oil over medium heat; cook onion, garlic and thyme, stirring occasionally, until onion is softened and light golden, about 5 minutes. Add spinach; cook, stirring, until wilted, about 2 minutes.

Meanwhile, in bowl, whisk together eggs, milk, salt and pepper; stir in turkey and ¼ cup of the Asiago. Pour over spinach mixture; reduce heat to medium-low. Cook, without stirring, until bottom and edge are set but top is still slightly runny, about 10 minutes.

Sprinkle with remaining ¼ cup Asiago. Broil until top is golden and set, about 3 minutes. Let stand for 3 minutes. Remove from skillet; cut into wedges.

NUTRITIONAL INFORMATION PER SERVING about 312 cal, 28 g pro, 19 g total fat (7 g sat. fat), 6 g carb (1 g dietary fibre, 3 g sugar), 404 mg chol, 453 mg sodium, 423 mg potassium. % RDI: 21% calcium, 24% iron, 53% vit A, 8% vit C, 47% folate.

TEST KITCHEN TIP

To remove your frittata from the skillet, first run a small knife around the edge to loosen it. Using a large spatula, lift it onto a cutting board to slice.

Greek Chicken Skillet

MAKES 4 SERVINGS
HANDS-ON TIME 20 MINUTES
TOTAL TIME 20 MINUTES

Place 1 chicken breast on cutting board. Holding knife blade parallel to board and with opposite hand on top of chicken, slice horizontally all the way through breast to form 2 thin cutlets; repeat with remaining breast. Using meat mallet or bottom of heavy pan, flatten chicken to even thickness. Sprinkle chicken all over with salt, pepper and garlic powder. Place flour in shallow dish; lightly coat each cutlet with flour, shaking off excess.

In large skillet, melt 1 tbsp of the butter over medium-high heat; cook chicken, turning once, until golden brown, 2 to 3 minutes. Transfer to plate.

In same pan, melt remaining 2 tbsp butter over medium heat; cook yellow pepper and red onion, stirring often, for 1 minute. Stir in tomatoes and rosemary; cook for 1 minute. Pour in wine, scraping up browned bits with wooden spoon. Add broth; bring to boil.

Return chicken to pan, partially nestling; add olives and capers. Reduce heat to medium; simmer, stirring often and turning chicken once, until chicken is no longer pink inside and sauce is slightly thickened, 5 to 8 minutes.

Sprinkle with Parmesan and parsley (if using).

NUTRITIONAL INFORMATION PER SERVING about 327 cal, 27 g pro, 17 g total fat (7 g sat. fat), 16 g carb (3 g dietary fibre, 5 g sugar), 81 mg chol, 932 mg sodium, 672 mg potassium. % RDI: 7% calcium, 12% iron, 17% vit A, 128% vit C, 16% folate.

2	boneless skinless chicken breasts (about 400 g total)
½ tsp	each salt and pepper
½ tsp	garlic powder
⅓ cup	all-purpose flour
3 tbsp	unsalted butter, divided
1	sweet yellow pepper, cut in chunks
quarter	large red onion, sliced
2 cups	cherry tomatoes
4	sprigs fresh rosemary
½ cup	dry white wine
1 cup	sodium-reduced chicken broth
20	Kalamata olives, pitted
2 tbsp	capers
¼ cup	shaved Parmesan cheese
¼ cup	coarsely chopped fresh parsley (optional)

Rosemary Steak, Mushrooms & Potatoes

MAKES 4 SERVINGS
HANDS-ON TIME 30 MINUTES
TOTAL TIME 30 MINUTES

12	mini yellow-fleshed potatoes, halved
2	strip loin grilling steaks, 1 inch thick (650 g total)
½ tsp	each salt, pepper and garlic powder
¼ cup	unsalted butter, divided
2	227 g pkgs white or cremini mushrooms
quarter	large red onion, sliced
2	sprigs fresh rosemary
1 tbsp	all-purpose flour
½ cup	dry red wine
1 cup	sodium-reduced beef broth

Place potatoes in microwaveable bowl; cover and microwave on high until fork-tender, 3 to 5 minutes. Set aside.

Sprinkle both sides of steaks with salt, pepper and garlic powder.

In large skillet, melt 2 tbsp of the butter over medium-high heat; cook steaks, turning once, until instant-read thermometer inserted sideways in centre reads 135°F for rare, 10 to 12 minutes. Transfer to cutting board; tent with foil.

In same pan, reduce heat to medium and melt remaining 2 tbsp butter. Add mushrooms, onion and rosemary; cook, stirring often, until mushrooms begin to brown, 8 to 10 minutes. Add flour; cook 1 minute more. Add wine, scraping up browned bits. Add broth; bring to boil. Return potatoes to pan and reduce heat to medium; simmer, stirring often, until sauce has thickened slightly, about 2 minutes. Slice steaks against grain and serve over potato mixture.

NUTRITIONAL INFORMATION PER SERVING about 520 cal, 36 g pro, 32 g total fat (16 g sat. fat), 19 g carb (3 g dietary fibre, 4 g sugar), 110 mg chol, 532 mg sodium, 1,112 mg potassium. % RDI: 4% calcium, 31% iron, 11% vit A, 15% vit C, 16% folate.

TEST KITCHEN TIP

To clean mushrooms, wipe with a damp kitchen towel or paper towels.

One-Pan Pork
With Veggies & Thyme

MAKES 4 SERVINGS
HANDS-ON TIME 25 MINUTES
TOTAL TIME 25 MINUTES

Place potatoes in microwaveable bowl; cover and microwave on high until fork-tender, 3 to 5 minutes. Set aside.

Sprinkle both sides of pork with salt, pepper and garlic powder. Dredge in flour; shake off excess.

In large skillet, melt 1 tbsp of the butter over medium-high heat; cook pork, turning once, until golden, 4 to 5 minutes. Transfer to plate.

In same pan, reduce heat to medium and melt remaining 2 tbsp butter. Add carrots, celery, onion and thyme sprigs; cook, stirring often, for 2 minutes. Add wine, scraping up browned bits. Add broth; bring to boil. Nestle pork into pan along with potatoes. Reduce heat to medium and simmer, stirring often and turning pork, until instant-read thermometer inserted sideways into centre of pork reads 155°F and sauce has thickened slightly, 8 to 10 minutes. Garnish with thyme leaves (if using).

NUTRITIONAL INFORMATION PER SERVING about 431 cal, 36 g pro, 22 g total fat (11 g sat. fat), 19 g carb (3 g dietary fibre, 4 g sugar), 104 mg chol, 562 mg sodium, 943 mg potassium. % RDI: 5% calcium, 15% iron, 84% vit A, 20% vit C, 13% folate.

12	mini yellow-fleshed potatoes, halved
4	boneless pork chops
½ tsp	each salt, pepper and garlic powder
⅓ cup	all-purpose flour
3 tbsp	unsalted butter, divided
2	large carrots, cut in thick julienne
2	ribs celery, thinly sliced
quarter	large red onion, sliced
8	sprigs fresh thyme
½ cup	dry white wine
1 cup	sodium-reduced chicken broth
1 tsp	fresh thyme leaves (optional)

Butter Chicken Mac & Cheese Skillet

MAKES 4 TO 6 SERVINGS
HANDS-ON TIME 20 MINUTES
TOTAL TIME 30 MINUTES

340 g	boneless skinless chicken breasts (about 3), cubed
pinch	each salt and pepper
¼ cup	butter, divided
half	onion, chopped
4 tsp	all-purpose flour
1½ cups	milk
½ cup	prepared butter chicken sauce
1¾ cups	shredded cheddar cheese, divided
1¾ cups	shredded mozzarella cheese, divided
1 tsp	tandoori masala (optional)
2 cups	elbow macaroni
¼ cup	chopped fresh cilantro

Sprinkle chicken with salt and pepper. In large cast-iron or ovenproof skillet, melt 1 tbsp of the butter over medium heat; cook chicken, stirring occasionally, until no longer pink inside, about 5 minutes. Transfer to bowl. Set aside.

In same pan, melt remaining 3 tbsp butter over medium heat; cook onion, stirring occasionally, until softened, about 2 minutes. Sprinkle in flour; cook, stirring, for 30 seconds. Gradually whisk in milk and butter chicken sauce; cook, whisking, until thick enough to coat back of spoon, about 4 minutes. Stir in 1½ cups each of the cheddar and mozzarella until melted. Stir in chicken and tandoori masala (if using).

Meanwhile, in large pot of boiling salted water, cook pasta according to package directions for al dente; drain well.

Stir pasta into chicken mixture until coated. Sprinkle with remaining ¼ cup each cheddar and mozzarella; broil until top is bubbling and lightly browned, about 3 minutes. Let stand for 4 minutes. Sprinkle with cilantro.

NUTRITIONAL INFORMATION PER EACH OF 6 SERVINGS about 569 cal, 36 g pro, 31 g total fat (19 g sat. fat), 35 g carb (1 g dietary fibre, 6 g sugar), 123 mg chol, 653 mg sodium, 370 mg potassium. % RDI: 47% calcium, 13% iron, 27% vit A, 2% vit C, 44% folate.

TEST KITCHEN TIP

Tandoori masala is a blend of garam masala, garlic and onion powders, ground ginger and cayenne pepper. Look for it in the spice aisle of your grocery store.

Mexican-Style Flatbreads

MAKES 4 SERVINGS
HANDS-ON TIME 25 MINUTES
TOTAL TIME 25 MINUTES

In nonstick skillet, heat oil over medium heat; cook onion, stirring often, until softened, about 7 minutes. Add beef; cook, breaking up with spoon, until browned on the outside but not cooked through, about 2 minutes. Add garlic, chili powder, coriander, cumin and salt; cook, stirring, until beef is no longer pink, about 3 minutes.

Add corn, 2 tbsp of the sour cream and the water; cook, stirring, until corn is heated through and mixture thickens slightly, about 2 minutes. Stir in ¼ cup of the cilantro.

Spoon beef mixture over cut sides of pitas; top with tomato, lettuce and remaining 1 tbsp sour cream and ¼ cup cilantro.

NUTRITIONAL INFORMATION PER SERVING about 375 cal, 24 g pro, 18 g total fat (6 g sat. fat), 32 g carb (3 g dietary fibre, 4 g sugar), 55 mg chol, 413 mg sodium, 522 mg potassium. % RDI: 6% calcium, 26% iron, 9% vit A, 12% vit C, 15% folate.

2 tsp	olive oil
1	onion, sliced
340 g	lean ground beef
3	cloves garlic, minced
2 tsp	chili powder
½ tsp	each ground coriander and ground cumin
¼ tsp	salt
¾ cup	frozen corn kernels
3 tbsp	sour cream, divided
2 tbsp	water
½ cup	chopped fresh cilantro, divided
2	whole wheat pita pockets (6 inches), split horizontally and toasted
1	Roma tomato, seeded and chopped
1 cup	shredded iceberg lettuce

Salmon Fillets
With Broccoli & Beans

MAKES 4 SERVINGS
HANDS-ON TIME 20 MINUTES
TOTAL TIME 20 MINUTES

12	mini yellow-fleshed potatoes, halved
4	skinless salmon fillets (about 450 g total)
½ tsp	each salt, pepper and garlic powder
3 tbsp	unsalted butter, divided
2 cups	green beans, trimmed and halved
quarter	large red onion, sliced
1 tbsp	all-purpose flour
½ cup	dry white wine
1 cup	sodium-reduced chicken broth
2 cups	broccoli florets
¼ cup	chopped fresh parsley
1	lemon, cut in wedges

Place potatoes in microwaveable bowl; cover and microwave on high until fork-tender, 3 to 5 minutes. Set aside.

Sprinkle both sides of fish with salt, pepper and garlic powder.

In large skillet, melt 1 tbsp of the butter over medium-high heat; cook fish, turning once, until golden, 2 to 3 minutes. Transfer to plate.

In same pan, reduce heat to medium and melt remaining 2 tbsp butter. Add beans and onion; cook, stirring often, for 1 minute. Add flour and cook for 1 minute. Add wine, scraping up browned bits. Add broth and broccoli; bring to boil and cook for 2 minutes. Nestle fish into pan along with potatoes. Reduce heat to medium and simmer, stirring often and turning fish, until fish flakes easily when tested and sauce has thickened slightly, 5 to 7 minutes. Sprinkle with parsley and serve with lemon wedges.

NUTRITIONAL INFORMATION PER SERVING 419 cal, 28 g pro, 24 g total fat (9 g sat. fat), 22 g carb (4 g dietary fibre, 5 g sugar), 85 mg chol, 522 mg sodium, 938 mg potassium. % RDI: 23% calcium, 13% iron, 201% vit A, 72% vit C, 45% folate.

Rustic Cannellini Bean & Vegetable Skillet

MAKES 4 SERVINGS
HANDS-ON TIME 30 MINUTES
TOTAL TIME 30 MINUTES

Place potatoes in microwaveable bowl; cover and microwave on high until fork-tender, 3 to 5 minutes. Set aside.

In large skillet, melt 1 tbsp of the butter over medium-high heat. Add baguette slices and cook for 5 minutes, turning once, until golden. Transfer to plate.

In same pan, reduce heat to medium and melt remaining 2 tbsp butter. Add onion and sage; cook for 2 minutes. Add tomatoes, salt, pepper, garlic powder and ½ cup of the broth; cook until tomatoes begin to soften, 3 to 4 minutes. Add remaining 1 cup broth; bring to boil.

Coarsely mash half of beans with fork. Add beans, kale, olives and potatoes to pan; reduce heat to medium and simmer, until sauce has thickened slightly, 4 to 6 minutes. Sprinkle with Parmesan and serve with baguette slices.

NUTRITIONAL INFORMATION PER SERVING about 410 cal, 14 g pro, 17 g total fat (7 g sat. fat), 54 g carb (9 g dietary fibre, 6 g sugar), 25 mg chol, 1,147 mg sodium, 726 mg potassium. % RDI: 13% calcium, 30% iron, 26% vit A, 40% vit C, 30% folate.

12	mini yellow-fleshed potatoes, halved
3 tbsp	unsalted butter, divided
4	slices (½ inch thick) baguette
quarter	large red onion, sliced
8	sage leaves, chopped
2	large plum tomatoes, each cut in 8 wedges
½ tsp	each salt, pepper and garlic powder
1½ cups	sodium-reduced vegetable broth, divided
1	540 ml can no-salt-added cannellini beans, drained and rinsed
4	cups packed chopped kale
20	pitted Kalamata olives
¼ cup	shaved Parmesan cheese

TEST KITCHEN TIP

Canned beans are a terrific timesaver, but many are high in sodium. Look for no-salt-added beans, which allow you much more control over the flavour and salt content of your family's meals.

MAKES 4 SERVINGS
HANDS-ON TIME 30 MINUTES
TOTAL TIME 45 MINUTES

Chicken Biryani

1 tsp	olive oil
4	bone-in skin-on chicken thighs (about 450 g total)
1	small sweet onion, diced
2 cups	chicken broth
1 cup	basmati rice, rinsed
1 tbsp	curry paste
1 tsp	ground cardamom
½ tsp	ground cloves
¼ tsp	salt
⅓ cup	dried apricots, thinly sliced
⅓ cup	roasted cashews
⅓ cup	roasted pumpkin seeds
¼ cup	dried black currants or sultana raisins
¼ cup	chopped fresh cilantro
¼ cup	chopped fresh mint
2 tbsp	crispy fried onions (optional)

In medium skillet, heat oil over medium-high heat and cook chicken, turning occasionally, until golden, about 7 minutes. Transfer to a plate.

Drain all but 1 tbsp fat from pan. Reduce heat to medium-low; add onion and cook, stirring occasionally, until lightly browned, 2 to 3 minutes. Stir in broth, rice, curry paste, cardamom, cloves and salt, stirring to combine.

Place chicken skin side up over rice and simmer, covered, on low heat until liquid is absorbed and juices run clear when thickest part of chicken is pierced, 12 to 15 minutes. Transfer chicken back to plate. Fluff rice with fork; stir in apricots, cashews, pumpkin seeds, black currants, cilantro and mint. Serve chicken on top of rice. Top with crispy onions (if using).

NUTRITIONAL INFORMATION PER SERVING about 610 cal, 26 g pro, 29 g total fat (7 g sat. fat), 61 g carb (4 g dietary fibre, 16 g sugar), 78 mg chol, 796 mg sodium, 675 mg potassium. % RDI: 7% calcium, 27% iron, 9% vit A, 8% vit C, 14% folate.

Shrimp Fried Rice

MAKES 6 TO 8 SERVINGS
HANDS-ON TIME 30 MINUTES
TOTAL TIME 30 MINUTES

In small bowl, whisk together soy sauce, ginger and sesame oil; set aside.

In large nonstick skillet, cook bacon over medium heat, stirring occasionally, until lightly crisp, 6 to 7 minutes. Using slotted spoon, transfer bacon to paper towel–lined plate; set aside.

In same pan, heat vegetable oil over medium-high heat; cook white parts of green onions and the garlic, stirring, for 30 seconds. Add shrimp; cook, stirring frequently, until pink and opaque throughout, 2 to 3 minutes. Add rice, pineapple, peas, bacon and soy sauce mixture; cook, stirring, until combined and warmed through, about 2 minutes. Sprinkle with green parts of green onions and the cashews (if using).

NUTRITIONAL INFORMATION PER EACH OF 8 SERVINGS about 256 cal, 9 g pro, 10 g total fat (2 g sat. fat), 33 g carb (2 g dietary fibre, 5 g sugar), 36 mg chol, 420 mg sodium, 215 mg potassium. % RDI: 4% calcium, 10% iron, 6% vit A, 23% vit C, 11% folate.

¼ cup	sodium-reduced soy sauce
1 tbsp	fresh ginger, minced
1 tsp	sesame oil
3	strips bacon, chopped
2 tbsp	vegetable oil
8	green onions, chopped (white and green parts separated)
2	cloves garlic, minced
200 g	large shrimp (31 to 40 count), peeled and deveined
5 cups	cooked white or brown rice
2 cups	chopped pineapple
1 cup	frozen peas, thawed
⅓ cup	chopped roasted cashews (optional)

TEST KITCHEN TIP

When making fried rice, don't use freshly made rice; it becomes sticky and mushy when fried. For best results, use rice that has been cooked the day before and refrigerated. And when you make rice in advance for fried rice, reduce the amount of water slightly to help keep the grains separate.

MAKES 4 SERVINGS
HANDS-ON TIME 10 MINUTES
TOTAL TIME 30 MINUTES

Chicken Chorizo Paella

¼ **tsp**	crumbled saffron threads
¾ **cup**	warm sodium-reduced chicken broth
¼ **tsp**	salt
450 **g**	boneless skinless chicken thighs, cut in bite-size pieces
2 **tbsp**	olive oil, divided
half	onion, diced
half	sweet red pepper, diced
1	clove garlic, minced
1 **tsp**	tomato paste
1 **cup**	arborio rice
¾ **cup**	water
½ **cup**	dry white wine
115 **g**	chorizo sausage, sliced
¼ **tsp**	smoked paprika
2 **tbsp**	minced fresh parsley

Stir saffron into broth; let stand for 10 minutes. Meanwhile, sprinkle salt over chicken. In large skillet, heat 1 tbsp of the oil over medium-high heat; cook chicken, turning occasionally, until golden. Transfer to plate.

Add remaining 1 tbsp oil to pan; cook onion and red pepper over low heat until onion is softened, about 10 minutes.

Stir in garlic and tomato paste; cook for 30 seconds. Stir in rice; cook, stirring, for 1 minute.

Add saffron broth, water, wine, chorizo and paprika. Return chicken to pan; bring to boil. Cover and cook over medium-low heat until rice is tender and no liquid remains, about 20 minutes. Stir in parsley. Let stand for 5 minutes.

NUTRITIONAL INFORMATION PER SERVING about 536 cal, 33 g pro, 24 g total fat (7 g sat. fat), 44 g carb (1 g dietary fibre), 119 mg chol, 708 mg sodium, 516 mg potassium. % RDI: 3% calcium, 17% iron, 11% vit A, 50% vit C, 8% folate.

TEST KITCHEN TIP

When buying saffron, look for crimson threads with a fresh, strong aroma and a recent harvest date. Unless you use it frequently, buy small amounts; most recipes use ¼ tsp or less, and saffron loses flavour with age. Store saffron as you would other spices: in an airtight container in a cool, dark place.

Ginger Orange Steaks
With Apricot Couscous

MAKES 4 SERVINGS
HANDS-ON TIME 25 MINUTES
TOTAL TIME 30 MINUTES

GINGER ORANGE STEAKS Sprinkle steaks with salt and pepper. In Dutch oven or large heavy-bottomed pot, heat 1 tbsp of the oil over medium heat; cook steaks, turning once, until desired doneness, 8 to 10 minutes for medium-rare. Transfer to plate; tent with foil.

In same pot, heat remaining 1 tbsp oil over medium heat; cook garlic and ginger, stirring, until fragrant, about 30 seconds. Add broth, orange juice and mustard, stirring and scraping up any browned bits; bring to boil. Reduce heat and simmer, stirring occasionally, until reduced by half, about 5 minutes. Scrape into serving dish; keep warm. Drizzle over steaks before serving.

APRICOT COUSCOUS In same pot, bring broth to boil. Add broccoli; cook, stirring, for 1 minute. Remove from heat; stir in couscous, apricots, salt and pepper. Cover and let stand until liquid is absorbed, about 5 minutes. Fluff with fork; serve with steaks.

NUTRITIONAL INFORMATION PER SERVING about 465 cal, 31 g pro, 16 g total fat (4 g sat. fat), 50 g carb (4 g dietary fibre, 15 g sugar), 55 mg chol, 583 mg sodium, 787 mg potassium. % RDI: 7% calcium, 26% iron, 11% vit A, 102% vit C, 32% folate.

GINGER ORANGE STEAKS

4	beef top sirloin grilling steak medallions (each about 150 g)
pinch	each salt and pepper
2 tbsp	olive oil, divided
2	cloves garlic, minced
2 tsp	minced peeled fresh ginger
¾ cup	sodium-reduced beef broth
⅓ cup	orange juice
1 tsp	Dijon mustard

APRICOT COUSCOUS

1½ cups	sodium-reduced beef broth
2 cups	frozen broccoli florets
1 cup	couscous
¼ cup	diced dried apricots
¼ tsp	each salt and pepper

MAKES 4 SERVINGS
HANDS-ON TIME 20 MINUTES
TOTAL TIME 35 MINUTES

Bean & Potato Skillet

4½ tbsp	olive oil, divided
1	onion, thinly sliced
1	large yellow-fleshed potato, scrubbed and diced
¾ tsp	salt, divided
¾ tsp	smoked paprika or paprika
4 cups	thinly sliced cabbage
1 tbsp	white wine vinegar
1	540 ml can navy beans, drained and rinsed
4	eggs
½ cup	Balkan-style yogurt
¼ cup	chopped fresh dill
	lemon wedges

In large nonstick skillet, heat 4 tbsp of the oil over medium heat; cook onion, potato, all but a pinch of the salt and paprika, stirring occasionally, until vegetables begin to brown, about 7 minutes.

Stir in cabbage, vinegar and ⅓ cup water; cover and cook until cabbage is wilted and softened, about 5 minutes. Remove lid and cook until cabbage begins to brown and liquid is absorbed, about 5 minutes. Stir in beans; cook until potatoes and cabbage are tender, about 4 minutes.

Meanwhile, in separate nonstick skillet, heat remaining ½ tbsp oil over medium heat. Cook eggs, sprinkling with remaining pinch of salt, until whites are set but yolks are still runny, about 3 minutes. Combine yogurt and dill, reserving some dill for garnish.

Divide potato mixture among 4 plates; top each with yogurt mixture, 1 fried egg and dill. Serve with lemon wedges.

NUTRITIONAL INFORMATION PER SERVING about 432 cal, 18 g pro, 23 g total fat (5 g sat. fat), 41 g carb (8 g dietary fibre, 6 g sugar), 198 mg chol, 939 mg sodium, 855 mg potassium. % RDI: 13% calcium, 29% iron, 15% vit A, 45% vit C, 54% folate.

Beef & Pepper Black Bean Udon Noodles

MAKES 4 SERVINGS
HANDS-ON TIME 15 MINUTES
TOTAL TIME 15 MINUTES

Stir together water, black bean garlic sauce and cornstarch. Set aside.

In wok or large nonstick skillet, heat 2 tsp of the oil over medium-high heat. Add beef; cook, stirring, until no longer pink, about 2 minutes. Transfer to plate.

Add remaining 2 tsp oil to wok. Add onion, green pepper, red pepper and ginger; cook, stirring, until peppers are tender-crisp, about 2 minutes.

Meanwhile, in large pot of boiling water, cook noodles according to package directions; drain.

Add beef, noodles and black bean mixture to wok; cook, stirring, until sauce is thickened, about 1 minute.

NUTRITIONAL INFORMATION PER SERVING about 406 cal, 30 g pro, 15 g total fat (4 g sat. fat), 38 g carb (3 g dietary fibre, 4 g sugar), 53 mg chol, 914 mg sodium, 489 mg potassium. % RDI: 3% calcium, 27% iron, 9% vit A, 118% vit C, 7% folate.

½ **cup**	water
2 tbsp	black bean garlic sauce
1 tsp	cornstarch
4 tsp	vegetable oil, divided
450 g	beef flank marinating steak, cut crosswise in ⅛-inch thick slices
1	small onion, thinly sliced
1	sweet green pepper, thinly sliced
1	sweet red pepper, thinly sliced
1 tsp	minced fresh ginger
2	200 g pkgs fresh udon noodles

Crispy Tofu Stir-Fry
With Udon Noodles

MAKES 4 SERVINGS
HANDS-ON TIME 30 MINUTES
TOTAL TIME 30 MINUTES

1	420 g pkg firm tofu, drained and cut in ¾-inch cubes
1 tbsp	cornstarch
2 tbsp	vegetable oil
1	227 g pkg cremini mushrooms, thinly sliced
4	cloves garlic, minced
1 tbsp	grated peeled fresh ginger
3 cups	bite-size broccoli florets
¾ cup	water
3 tbsp	hoisin sauce
1 tsp	Asian chili sauce (such as sriracha)
3	200 g pkgs fresh udon noodles
2	green onions, thinly sliced
1 tsp	sesame oil

Pat tofu dry and toss gently with cornstarch to coat. In wok or large nonstick skillet, heat all but 2 tsp of the vegetable oil over medium-high heat; cook tofu, turning occasionally, until crisp and golden, 8 to 10 minutes. Remove to paper towel–lined plate to drain. Set aside.

In same pan, heat remaining 2 tsp vegetable oil over medium-high heat; stir-fry mushrooms, garlic and ginger until mushrooms are beginning to soften, about 2 minutes. Add broccoli; stir-fry until tender-crisp, about 3 minutes. Stir in water, hoisin sauce and chili sauce; bring to boil.

Reduce heat to low; add noodles, tossing gently to coat. Simmer, stirring gently, until sauce is slightly thickened, about 2 minutes. Add tofu, green onions and sesame oil; cook, tossing to coat, for 1 minute.

NUTRITIONAL INFORMATION PER SERVING about 515 cal, 28 g pro, 17 g total fat (2 g sat. fat), 68 g carb (5 g dietary fibre, 6 g sugar), 0 mg chol, 261 mg sodium, 717 mg potassium. % RDI: 20% calcium, 41% iron, 16% vit A, 53% vit C, 26% folate.

TEST KITCHEN TIP

You can replace the tofu with cubed pork or chicken, if you prefer.

Ham & Napa Cabbage Stir-Fry

MAKES 4 SERVINGS
HANDS-ON TIME 15 MINUTES
TOTAL TIME 15 MINUTES

In glass measure or small bowl, whisk together broth, cornstarch, vinegar, honey, five-spice powder, salt and ¼ cup water. Set aside.

In wok or large nonstick skillet, heat oil over medium-high heat; stir-fry white parts of green onions, the garlic and ginger for 1 minute. Add cabbage and ham; stir-fry until cabbage is tender-crisp, about 3 minutes.

Stir in broth mixture; bring to boil. Cook, stirring, until coated and sauce is thickened, 1 to 2 minutes. Sprinkle with green parts of green onions.

NUTRITIONAL INFORMATION PER SERVING about 170 cal, 11 g pro, 10 g total fat (2 g sat. fat), 9 g carb (2 g dietary fibre, 4 g sugar), 25 mg chol, 691 mg sodium, 270 mg potassium. % RDI: 4% calcium, 11% iron, 3% vit A, 7% vit C, 19% folate.

½ cup	sodium-reduced chicken broth
1 tbsp	cornstarch
1 tbsp	rice vinegar
2 tsp	liquid honey
½ tsp	five-spice powder
pinch	salt
2 tbsp	vegetable oil
3	green onions, sliced (white and green parts separated)
2	cloves garlic, thinly sliced
1 tbsp	minced fresh ginger
6 cups	coarsely chopped napa cabbage (about half a head)
1¼ cups	thinly sliced fully cooked ham, cut in strips or shredded

TEST KITCHEN TIP

This recipe is an easy way to use leftover ham for a quick weeknight supper, but you don't need to wait for leftovers; just pick up some cooked ham at the deli counter.

Thai Veggie Curry

MAKES 4 SERVINGS
HANDS-ON TIME 35 MINUTES
TOTAL TIME 35 MINUTES

⅓ cup	unsalted cashews
2 tsp	vegetable oil
2	cloves garlic, minced
3 tbsp	Thai red curry paste
1	400 ml can coconut milk
½ cup	water
2 tsp	grated lime zest
¼ cup	lime juice
1 tbsp	packed brown sugar
½ tsp	salt (optional)
3	heads baby bok choy, quartered lengthwise
3	200 g pkgs cooked udon noodles
1	large carrot, julienned
4	lime wedges (optional)
	Thai basil leaves (optional)

In large dry skillet or wok, toast cashews over medium-high heat until fragrant, 1 to 2 minutes. Transfer to cutting board; coarsely chop. Set aside.

In same pan, heat oil over medium heat; cook garlic for 30 seconds. Add curry paste; cook, stirring often, for 1 minute. Stir in coconut milk and water; bring to boil over high heat. Reduce heat to medium; simmer, stirring occasionally, for 5 minutes. Stir in lime zest, lime juice, brown sugar, salt (if using) and bok choy; cook, stirring occasionally, for 5 minutes. Add noodles; cook, gently stirring, until warmed through and curry is slightly thickened, 3 to 5 minutes. Divide among serving bowls; sprinkle with carrot and cashews. Garnish with lime wedges and basil (if using).

NUTRITIONAL INFORMATION PER SERVING about 523 cal, 12 g pro, 29 g total fat (19 g sat. fat), 61 g carb (5 g dietary fibre, 8 g sugar), 0 mg chol, 45 mg sodium, 535 mg potassium. % RDI: 11% calcium, 39% iron, 92% vit A, 35% vit C, 18% folate.

TEST KITCHEN TIP

Thai basil has a strong, spicy flavour and is available in Asian grocery stores. If you can't find it, regular basil makes a fine substitute.

Spicy Peanut Shrimp & Noodles

MAKES 2 TO 3 SERVINGS
HANDS-ON TIME 15 MINUTES
TOTAL TIME 25 MINUTES

In bowl, whisk together peanut butter, brown sugar, soy sauce, fish sauce, lime juice, vinegar and chili sauce until smooth; gradually whisk in broth until combined. Set aside.

Place noodles in large heatproof bowl; pour in enough boiling water to cover noodles. Let stand until noodles are pliable, about 15 minutes. Drain and rinse under cold water; drain again.

Meanwhile, in large nonstick skillet, heat oil over medium-high heat; cook garlic and ginger, stirring, until fragrant, about 30 seconds. Add shrimp; stir-fry until shrimp are pink and opaque throughout, 2 to 3 minutes.

Stir in broth mixture and noodles until coated. Remove from heat. Add snap peas; toss to combine. Sprinkle with peanuts. Serve with lime wedges.

NUTRITIONAL INFORMATION PER EACH OF 3 SERVINGS about 625 cal, 27 g pro, 17 g total fat (3 g sat. fat), 90 g carb (5 g dietary fibre, 13 g sugar), 115 mg chol, 887 mg sodium, 444 mg potassium. % RDI: 9% calcium, 25% iron, 6% vit A, 21% vit C, 23% folate.

¼ cup	smooth peanut butter
2 tbsp	packed brown sugar
1 tbsp	sodium-reduced soy sauce
1 tbsp	fish sauce
1 tbsp	lime juice
1 tbsp	unseasoned rice vinegar
2 tsp	Asian chili sauce (such as sriracha)
½ cup	sodium-reduced chicken broth
260 g	rice stick noodles (¼ inch wide)
	boiling water
1 tsp	vegetable oil
2	cloves garlic, minced
1 tsp	grated fresh ginger
170 g	jumbo shrimp (21 to 25 count), peeled and deveined
1 cup	sugar snap peas, trimmed
2 tbsp	chopped salted roasted peanuts
	lime wedges

TEST KITCHEN TIP

Look for the shrimp "count" on the package label; it means the number of shrimp that make up one pound. Count is a more accurate indicator of size than terms like "large" or "jumbo," which are used inconsistently.

MAKES 4 TO 6 SERVINGS
HANDS-ON TIME 30 MINUTES
TOTAL TIME 50 MINUTES

Singapore Noodles

225 g	pork tenderloin, trimmed and sliced in thin strips
2 tbsp	sodium-reduced soy sauce, divided
1 tsp	sesame oil
½ tsp	salt, divided
¼ tsp	pepper
280 g	dried rice vermicelli
	boiling water
4 tsp	vegetable oil, divided
2	eggs, lightly beaten
225 g	jumbo shrimp (21 to 25 count), peeled and deveined
1	small onion, thinly sliced
half	sweet red pepper, thinly sliced
2	cloves garlic, minced
2	green onions, cut in 1½-inch lengths
2 tsp	curry powder
1 tsp	turmeric
1 tsp	granulated sugar
2 cups	bean sprouts

In bowl, stir together pork, 2 tsp of the soy sauce, the sesame oil, pinch of the salt and the pepper. Cover and refrigerate for 30 minutes. *(Make-ahead: Refrigerate for up to 24 hours.)*

Meanwhile, place vermicelli in large heatproof bowl; add enough boiling water to cover, and soak according to package directions. Drain and rinse under cold water; drain well.

In wok or large nonstick skillet, heat 1 tsp of the vegetable oil over medium-high heat; cook eggs, stirring, just until set, about 1 minute. Scrape onto plate. Wipe out pan. Add 1 tsp of the remaining vegetable oil to pan. Add shrimp; cook over medium-high heat, stirring, until pink and opaque throughout, about 2 minutes. Transfer to plate. Add 1 tsp of the remaining vegetable oil to pan. Add pork mixture; cook over medium-high heat, stirring, until just a hint of pink remains inside, about 3 minutes. Transfer to plate.

Add remaining 1 tsp vegetable oil to wok. Add onion, red pepper and garlic; cook over medium-high heat, stirring, until pepper is tender-crisp, about 2 minutes. Add vermicelli, egg, shrimp, pork, green onions, curry powder, turmeric, sugar and remaining soy sauce and salt. Cook, stirring and tossing, until well combined and heated through, about 3 minutes. Add bean sprouts; cook, stirring, until softened, about 1 minute.

NUTRITIONAL INFORMATION PER EACH OF 6 SERVINGS about 330 cal, 19 g pro, 7 g total fat (1 g sat. fat), 46 g carb (3 g dietary fibre, 4 g sugar), 124 mg chol, 504 mg sodium, 328 mg potassium. % RDI: 4% calcium, 18% iron, 8% vit A, 37% vit C, 18% folate.

VARIATION

Vegetarian Singapore Noodles
Omit shrimp. Replace pork with one 350 g pkg extra-firm tofu, drained and cut in ½-inch cubes.

Spring Pea Spaghetti Carbonara

MAKES 4 SERVINGS
HANDS-ON TIME 25 MINUTES
TOTAL TIME 25 MINUTES

225 g	spaghetti
6	strips bacon, cut in chunks
2 cups	fresh green peas
6	egg yolks
1 cup	finely grated Parmesan or Pecorino-Romano cheese, divided
1 tsp	pepper
¼ tsp	salt
1 cup	pea shoots (optional)

In large pot of boiling water, cook pasta according to package directions. Reserving 1 cup of the cooking liquid, drain.

Meanwhile, in large nonstick skillet, cook bacon over medium heat, stirring occasionally, until crisp, 6 to 8 minutes. Using slotted spoon, transfer bacon to paper towel–lined plate.

Drain all but 2 tbsp fat from pan. Return half of the bacon to pan; add peas and cook over medium heat, stirring, until heated through, about 1 minute. Remove from heat. Add pasta and ½ cup of the cooking liquid; toss to coat.

In bowl, whisk egg yolks with ¾ cup of the Parmesan. Working quickly, scrape egg yolk mixture, pepper and salt into pasta mixture; toss until sauce is thickened, adding additional cooking liquid if needed to reach desired consistency. Divide among serving plates; sprinkle with remaining ¼ cup Parmesan and the bacon. Top with pea shoots (if using).

NUTRITIONAL INFORMATION PER SERVING about 531 cal, 25 g pro, 24 g total fat (9 g sat. fat), 54 g carb (6 g dietary fibre, 5 g sugar), 317 mg chol, 890 mg sodium, 372 mg potassium. % RDI: 17% calcium, 31% iron, 22% vit A, 17% vit C, 97% folate.

TEST KITCHEN TIP

To portion out 225 grams of uncooked spaghetti, hold it in your fist; the correct amount will measure 1¼ inches in diameter.

One-Pot Pasta
With Shrimp, Tomatoes & Feta

MAKES 4 TO 6 SERVINGS
HANDS-ON TIME 20 MINUTES
TOTAL TIME 20 MINUTES

340 g	spaghetti
2 tbsp	olive oil
4	cloves garlic, sliced
1 tsp	dried oregano
¼ tsp	hot pepper flakes
450 g	jumbo shrimp (21 to 25 count), peeled and deveined
half	red onion, sliced
3 cups	halved cherry tomatoes (about 475 g total)
¼ cup	pitted Kalamata olives, chopped
⅓ cup	chopped fresh parsley
¼ cup	crumbled feta cheese

In large pot of boiling lightly salted water, cook pasta according to package directions. Reserving ½ cup of the cooking liquid, drain. Set aside.

In same pot, heat oil over medium heat; cook garlic, oregano and hot pepper flakes, stirring, until fragrant, about 30 seconds. Add shrimp and red onion; cook, stirring, until shrimp are beginning to turn pink, about 1 minute. Add tomatoes and olives; cook, stirring occasionally, until shrimp are pink and opaque throughout and tomatoes are beginning to soften, about 2 minutes.

Stir in pasta, parsley and reserved cooking liquid; cook for 1 minute. Top with feta.

NUTRITIONAL INFORMATION PER EACH OF 6 SERVINGS about 374 cal, 22 g pro, 10 g total fat (2 g sat. fat), 50 g carb (3 g dietary fibre, 4 g sugar), 91 mg chol, 490 mg sodium, 424 mg potassium. % RDI: 9% calcium, 27% iron, 13% vit A, 27% vit C, 69% folate.

TEST KITCHEN TIP

Reserving a little of the cooking liquid is a useful technique for many pasta recipes. The starch in the liquid helps sauce ingredients adhere to the pasta, and the liquid can also loosen up a sauce that's thickened too much.

Mushroom & Parmesan Linguine

MAKES 4 SERVINGS
HANDS-ON TIME 15 MINUTES
TOTAL TIME 15 MINUTES

In large pot of boiling lightly salted water, cook pasta according to package directions until al dente. Reserving ⅓ cup of the cooking liquid, drain.

Meanwhile, in large nonstick skillet, melt butter over medium-high heat; sauté garlic until fragrant, about 1 minute. Add cremini and shiitake mushrooms and thyme; sauté until just softened, about 3 minutes.

Stir in pasta, reserved cooking liquid, Parmesan cheese, cream, lemon zest, lemon juice and pepper; cook, stirring, until sauce is slightly thickened, about 1 minute. Stir in parsley.

NUTRITIONAL INFORMATION PER SERVING about 568 cal, 25 g pro, 20 g total fat (12 g sat. fat), 72 g carb (5 g dietary fibre, 3 g sugar), 58 mg chol, 724 mg sodium, 525 mg potassium. % RDI: 30% calcium, 25% iron, 14% vit A, 13% vit C, 95% folate.

340 g	linguine
4 tsp	butter
6	cloves garlic, minced
1	227 g pkg cremini mushrooms, thinly sliced
2 cups	sliced shiitake mushrooms (about 125 g)
1 tsp	chopped fresh thyme
1 cup	grated Parmesan cheese
⅓ cup	35% cream
2 tsp	grated lemon zest
2 tbsp	lemon juice
½ tsp	pepper
2 tbsp	chopped fresh parsley

TEST KITCHEN TIP

Mushrooms cook faster when spread over a large surface, so choose your largest nonstick skillet.

Spinach & Herb Chickpea Linguine

MAKES 4 SERVINGS
HANDS-ON TIME 35 MINUTES
TOTAL TIME 35 MINUTES

¼ **cup**	olive oil (approx)
1	540 ml can chickpeas, drained, rinsed and patted dry
½ **tsp**	each salt and pepper
3	cloves garlic, minced
½ **tsp**	hot pepper flakes (optional)
200 **g**	linguine
8 **cups**	baby spinach
1 **cup**	packed fresh parsley leaves, chopped
1 **cup**	packed fresh basil leaves, chopped
1 **cup**	finely grated Parmesan cheese (approx)
1 **tbsp**	lemon zest
3 **tbsp**	lemon juice

In large skillet, heat oil over medium heat; cook chickpeas, salt and pepper, stirring occasionally, until chickpeas are crisp and beginning to split, about 15 minutes. Increase heat to medium-high; cook chickpeas, stirring, until browned, about 5 minutes. Stir in garlic and hot pepper flakes (if using); cook until fragrant, about 1 minute.

Meanwhile, in large pot of boiling water, cook pasta according to package directions. Reserving 1 cup of the cooking liquid, drain.

Reserve ½ cup of the chickpea mixture for garnish. Add pasta and reserved cooking liquid to remaining chickpea mixture; toss to combine. Add spinach, parsley, basil, Parmesan, lemon zest and lemon juice; toss to coat.

Divide among serving plates; top with reserved chickpea mixture. Drizzle with additional olive oil and sprinkle with additional Parmesan, if desired.

NUTRITIONAL INFORMATION PER SERVING about 480 cal, 18 g pro, 20 g total fat (4 g sat. fat), 59 g carb (8 g dietary fibre, 4 g sugar), 8 mg chol, 660 mg sodium, 375 mg potassium. % RDI: 22% calcium, 31% iron, 41% vit A, 35% vit C, 92% folate.

TEST KITCHEN TIP

Try other combinations of fresh tender herbs in place of the parsley and basil: Chives, cilantro and dill are all good choices.

Mushroom & Spinach Bow Ties

MAKES 4 SERVINGS
HANDS-ON TIME 20 MINUTES
TOTAL TIME 30 MINUTES

In large pot of boiling salted water, cook pasta according to package directions. Reserving 1 cup of the cooking liquid, drain.

Meanwhile, in large nonstick skillet, melt 2 tbsp of the butter over medium-high heat. Add mushrooms; cook, stirring frequently, until tender and golden, about 8 minutes. Add garlic, thyme, pepper and salt during last minute of cooking.

Add wine; bring to boil. Reduce heat and simmer, stirring often, until liquid is reduced by half, 3 to 5 minutes. Transfer mushroom mixture to pot used to cook pasta; place over medium heat. Stir in pasta, ½ cup of the cooking liquid and remaining 1 tbsp butter; gradually stir in Parmesan until pasta is evenly coated. Stir in spinach, a few handfuls at a time, just until wilted. Add remaining ½ cup cooking liquid; sprinkle with more salt and Parmesan, if desired.

NUTRITIONAL INFORMATION PER SERVING about 434 cal, 18 g pro, 13 g total fat (7 g sat. fat), 58 g carb (6 g dietary fibre, 4 g sugar), 28 mg chol, 583 mg sodium, 969 mg potassium. % RDI: 21% calcium, 45% iron, 84% vit A, 13% vit C, 120% folate.

half	500 g pkg bow tie pasta (about 4 cups)
3 tbsp	unsalted butter, divided
500 g	mixed mushrooms, thinly sliced
3	cloves garlic, finely grated or pressed
1½ tsp	dried thyme
½ tsp	pepper
¼ tsp	salt (approx)
1 cup	dry white wine (such as Sauvignon Blanc)
1 cup	grated Parmesan cheese (approx)
10 cups	lightly packed baby spinach

MAKES 8 SERVINGS
HANDS-ON TIME 20 MINUTES
COOKING TIME 6¼ HOURS
TOTAL TIME 6½ HOURS

Slow Cooker Tomato & Sausage Pasta

4	mild Italian sausages (about 400 g total), casings removed and broken in bite-size pieces
1	onion, sliced
1	eggplant, chopped in ¾-inch pieces
1	227 g pkg cremini mushrooms, sliced
3	cloves garlic, sliced
1	660 ml bottle strained tomatoes (passata)
2 tbsp	tomato paste
2 tsp	balsamic vinegar
1 tsp	Italian herb seasoning
¼ tsp	hot pepper flakes
pinch	each salt and pepper
1 tbsp	all-purpose flour
1 tbsp	water
700 g	fusilli
½ cup	grated Parmesan cheese
¼ cup	fresh basil leaves, torn

In slow cooker, combine sausages, onion, eggplant, mushrooms and garlic; stir in strained tomatoes, tomato paste, vinegar, Italian seasoning, hot pepper flakes, salt and pepper. Cover and cook on low heat until sausage is cooked through and eggplant is tender, 6 to 8 hours.

Whisk flour with water until smooth; whisk into slow cooker. Cover and cook on high until slightly thickened, about 10 minutes. *(Make-ahead: Let cool for 30 minutes. Refrigerate in airtight container for up to 3 days.)*

Meanwhile, in large pot of boiling salted water, cook pasta according to package directions until al dente; drain. Spoon sauce over pasta; top with Parmesan and basil.

NUTRITIONAL INFORMATION PER SERVING about 535 cal, 22 g pro, 14 g total fat (5 g sat. fat), 79 g carb (5 g dietary fibre, 8 g sugar), 27 mg chol, 818 mg sodium, 630 mg potassium. % RDI: 11% calcium, 38% iron, 3% vit A, 8% vit C, 99% folate.

Zucchini & Chicken Alfredo

MAKES 6 SERVINGS
HANDS-ON TIME 25 MINUTES
TOTAL TIME 30 MINUTES

In large pot of boiling salted water, cook pasta according to package directions. Reserving ½ cup of the cooking liquid, drain.

Meanwhile, in large skillet, heat oil over medium heat. Add chicken and salt; cook, stirring occasionally, until browned, 3 to 4 minutes. Add zucchini; cook, stirring occasionally, until softened, about 2 minutes. Transfer to bowl; set aside.

In same skillet, add lemon juice. Cook, stirring and scraping up any browned bits, for 1 to 2 minutes. Add Parmesan, cream, thyme, pepper, and up to 1 tbsp more lemon juice to taste; cook, stirring frequently, until slightly thickened, 3 to 4 minutes. Stir in pasta, chicken and zucchini. If needed, add reserved cooking liquid, 1 tbsp at a time, to loosen sauce. Stir in lemon zest. Serve immediately.

NUTRITIONAL INFORMATION PER SERVING about 539 cal, 27 g pro, 25 g total fat (13 g sat. fat), 51 g carb (3 g dietary fibre, 2 g sugar), 109 mg chol, 609 mg sodium, 430 mg potassium. % RDI: 22% calcium, 22% iron, 24% vit A, 23% vit C, 75% folate.

375 g	rigatoni
1 tbsp	olive oil
4	boneless skinless chicken thighs, cut in ½-inch wide strips
¼ tsp	salt
2	small yellow or green zucchini, thinly sliced crosswise
2 tsp	grated lemon zest
2 tbsp	lemon juice (approx)
1 cup	grated Parmesan cheese
1 cup	35% cream
2 tbsp	chopped fresh thyme
½ tsp	pepper

TEST KITCHEN TIP

To punch up the flavour of this dish, stir in ½ tsp hot pepper flakes and a couple of finely grated or pressed garlic cloves with the lemon juice.

MAKES 4 SERVINGS
HANDS-ON TIME 15 MINUTES
TOTAL TIME 20 MINUTES

Creamy Broccoli Rotini

1	head broccoli (about 325 g)
340 g	rotini
1 tbsp	olive oil
3	cloves garlic, sliced
¾ cup	mascarpone cheese
1 tsp	lemon zest
2 tsp	lemon juice
¼ tsp	each salt and pepper

Cut stem from broccoli head; cut head into florets. Trim bottom end of stem; peel outer layer. Thinly slice stem. Set aside.

In large pot of boiling salted water, cook pasta according to package directions, adding broccoli florets and stem during last 2 minutes of cooking. Reserving 1 cup of the cooking liquid, drain.

In nonstick skillet, heat oil over medium heat; cook garlic, stirring, until fragrant, about 1 minute. Add mascarpone; cook, stirring occasionally, until melted. Stir in pasta mixture, lemon zest, tossing and adding enough of reserved cooking liquid to coat. Stir in lemon juice, salt and pepper.

NUTRITIONAL INFORMATION PER SERVING about 553 cal, 19 g pro, 21 g total fat (11 g sat. fat), 71 g carb (5 g dietary fibre, 3 g sugar), 39 mg chol, 761 mg sodium, 343 mg potassium. % RDI: 14% calcium, 24% iron, 21% vit A, 92% vit C, 127% folate.

TEST KITCHEN TIP

Stir any leftover mascarpone with a little honey and serve with fresh fruit for a speedy dessert.

Spinach & Sausage Skillet Lasagna

MAKES 8 TO 10 SERVINGS
HANDS-ON TIME 50 MINUTES
TOTAL TIME 1¼ HOURS

In deep 12-inch ovenproof skillet, heat oil over medium-high heat; cook onion, stirring, until softened, 2 to 3 minutes. Add beef, sausages and garlic; cook, stirring and breaking up with spoon, until beef and sausages are no longer pink, about 4 minutes.

Stir in tomato paste, ½ tsp of the salt and hot pepper flakes; cook, stirring occasionally, until slightly thickened, about 2 minutes. Stir in tomatoes. Reduce heat to medium; cook, stirring occasionally, until slightly thickened, 12 to 15 minutes. Scrape into large bowl; wipe pan clean.

Meanwhile, in bowl, stir together ricotta, spinach, egg, ¾ cup of the Parmesan and remaining ½ tsp salt.

In same pan, spread 1 cup of the meat sauce to coat bottom. Arrange 2 lasagna noodles over top; top with 1 cup of the remaining meat sauce and half of the ricotta mixture. Repeat layers; top with remaining lasagna noodles and meat sauce. Bring sauce to boil over high heat. Reduce heat to medium; cover and simmer until noodles are tender, 15 to 18 minutes.

Arrange rack in oven 6 inches from broiler. Sprinkle lasagna with mozzarella and remaining 1 cup Parmesan. Transfer to oven; broil until top is golden and cheese is melted, about 2 minutes. Let stand for 15 minutes. Sprinkle with basil leaves (if using) before serving.

NUTRITIONAL INFORMATION PER EACH OF 10 SERVINGS about 400 cal, 24 g pro, 20 g total fat (9 g sat. fat), 11 g carb (2 g dietary fibre, 5 g sugar), 74 mg chol, 782 mg sodium, 584 mg potassium. % RDI: 35% calcium, 22% iron, 14% vit A, 28% vit C, 36% folate.

2 tbsp	olive oil
1	onion, chopped
225 g	lean ground beef
200 g	mild Italian sausages (about 2), casings removed
4	cloves garlic, minced
2 tbsp	tomato paste
1 tsp	salt, divided
½ tsp	hot pepper flakes
1	796 ml can whole tomatoes, coarsely chopped
1	475 g tub extra-smooth ricotta cheese
1	300 g pkg frozen chopped spinach, thawed and squeezed dry
1	egg, beaten
1¾ cups	finely grated Parmesan cheese, divided
6	sheets (each 10 x 6 inches) fresh lasagna noodles
1 cup	shredded mozzarella cheese fresh basil leaves(optional)

TEST KITCHEN TIP

To chop canned whole tomatoes without creating a mess, use a pair of kitchen shears to cut them into chunks while still in the can.

Spinach & Avocado Green Goddess Pasta

MAKES 4 SERVINGS
HANDS-ON TIME 10 MINUTES
TOTAL TIME 25 MINUTES

3	cloves garlic, smashed
2	avocados, peeled and pitted
4 cups	packed baby spinach
⅓ cup	nutritional yeast
¼ cup	chopped fresh dill
¼ cup	each olive oil and cold water
2 tsp	grated lemon zest
3 tbsp	lemon juice
1 tsp	salt
¼ tsp	pepper
500 g	rigatoni or farfalle
1	bunch (about 450 g) asparagus, trimmed and cut in 2-inch lengths

In food processor, pulse together garlic, avocados, spinach, nutritional yeast, dill, oil, water, lemon zest, lemon juice, salt and pepper until smooth. Mixture will resemble pesto. Set aside.

In large pot of boiling salted water, cook pasta according to package directions. Add asparagus during last 4 minutes of cooking. Reserving ¼ cup of the cooking liquid, drain pasta and asparagus. Return to pot; gently stir in pesto until combined. If needed, gradually stir in enough of the reserved cooking liquid to loosen sauce. Garnish with sprigs of fresh dill and sprinkle with more nutritional yeast, if you wish.

NUTRITIONAL INFORMATION PER SERVING about 757 cal, 24 g pro, 27 g total fat (4 g sat. fat), 107 g carb (12 g dietary fibre, 4 g sugar), 0 mg chol, 1,196 mg sodium, 890 mg potassium. % RDI: 8% calcium, 45% iron, 38% vit A, 47% vit C, 279% folate.

TEST KITCHEN TIP

Nutritional yeast is a good vegan source of protein and vitamin B with a rich cheese flavour reminiscent of Parmesan. If you can't find it in your grocery store, look for it in heath food stores and bulk food stores.

One-Pot Crab, Pea & Ricotta Spaghetti

MAKES 4 TO 6 SERVINGS
HANDS-ON TIME 15 MINUTES
TOTAL TIME 25 MINUTES

In large pot of boiling salted water, cook pasta according to package directions, adding peas during last 2 minutes of cooking. Reserving 1 cup of the cooking liquid, drain. Return pasta mixture to pot over medium-low heat.

Stir in ricotta, tarragon, oil, butter, lemon zest, lemon juice, Thai pepper, salt, pepper, nutmeg and enough of the reserved cooking liquid to loosen sauce; fold in crabmeat. Stir in up to 1 tbsp more tarragon and half Thai pepper, seeded and minced, if you wish. Cook until warmed through, about 3 minutes.

NUTRITIONAL INFORMATION PER EACH OF 6 SERVINGS about 457 cal, 26 g pro, 16 g total fat (7 g sat. fat), 52 g carb (3 g dietary fibre, 2 g sugar), 69 mg chol, 768 mg sodium, 348 mg potassium. % RDI: 12% calcium, 19% iron, 14% vit A, 10% vit C, 82% folate.

375 g	spaghetti
1 cup	fresh or frozen peas
1 cup	smooth ricotta cheese
2 tbsp	finely chopped fresh tarragon (approx)
2 tbsp	olive oil
2 tbsp	butter, softened
2 tsp	grated lemon zest
1 tbsp	lemon juice
half	Thai bird's-eye pepper, seeded and minced (approx)
½ tsp	salt
¼ tsp	pepper
pinch	nutmeg
1½ cups	shredded cooked crabmeat

MAKES 4 SERVINGS
HANDS-ON TIME 30 MINUTES
TOTAL TIME 30 MINUTES

Pork Tenderloin
With Mushroom Gravy & Egg Noodles

450 g	pork tenderloin, trimmed and cut in 1-inch thick rounds
¼ tsp	pepper
pinch	salt
1 tbsp	olive oil, divided
2	227 g pkgs cremini mushrooms, sliced
3	cloves garlic, minced
2 tsp	chopped fresh thyme
¾ cup	sodium-reduced chicken broth
¾ cup	water
2 tsp	cornstarch
2 tbsp	light sour cream
2 tsp	Dijon mustard
1 tsp	balsamic vinegar
2 tbsp	chopped fresh parsley
140 g	egg noodles
½ cup	frozen peas

Sprinkle pork with pepper and salt. In nonstick skillet, heat 1½ tsp of the oil over medium-high heat; cook pork, turning once, until browned, about 5 minutes. Transfer to plate; keep warm.

In same pan, heat remaining 1½ tsp oil over medium heat; cook mushrooms, garlic and thyme, stirring occasionally, until almost no liquid remains, about 6 minutes. Scrape into bowl; keep warm.

Whisk together broth, water and cornstarch; stir into pan. Bring to simmer; cook, scraping up browned bits, until thickened, about 5 minutes.

Return pork and any juices and mushroom mixture to skillet; cook, stirring, until sauce is glossy and thickened, about 3 minutes. Stir in sour cream, mustard and vinegar; cook until instant-read thermometer inserted sideways into centre of pork reads 155°F, about 2 minutes. Stir in parsley.

Meanwhile, in large pot of boiling lightly salted water, cook noodles according to package directions, adding peas in last 3 minutes of cooking time. Drain. Serve pork mixture over noodles and peas.

NUTRITIONAL INFORMATION PER SERVING about 345 cal, 33 g pro, 8 g total fat (2 g sat. fat), 35 g carb (5 g dietary fibre, 4 g sugar), 91 mg chol, 436 mg sodium, 1,011 mg potassium. % RDI: 6% calcium, 29% iron, 7% vit A, 10% vit C, 57% folate.

TEST KITCHEN TIP

Frozen peas need just enough time in the boiling water to thaw and heat through; adding them near the end of the cooking time helps preserve their bright green colour.

Index

About Our Nutrition Information

To meet nutrient needs each day, moderately active women aged 25 to 49 need about 1,900 calories, 51 g protein, 261 g carbohydrate, 25 to 35 g fibre and not more than 63 g total fat (21 g saturated fat). Men and teenagers usually need more. Canadian sodium intake of approximately 3,500 mg daily should be reduced, whereas the intake of potassium from food sources should be increased to 4,700 mg per day. The percentage of recommended daily intake (% RDI) is based on the values used for Canadian food labels for calcium, iron, vitamins A and C, and folate.

Figures are rounded off. They are based on the first ingredient listed when there is a choice and do not include optional ingredients or those with no specified amounts.

Abbreviations

cal = calories   **pro** = protein   **carb** = carbohydrate   **sat. fat** = saturated fat   **chol** = cholesterol

Canadian Living

Complete your collection of Tested-Till-Perfect recipes!

The Ultimate Cookbook
The Special Occasions Cookbook
New Slow Cooker Favourites

The Complete Chicken Cookbook
The Complete Chocolate Cookbook
The Complete Preserving Cookbook
The Complete Vegetarian Cookbook

400-Calorie Dinners
Dinner in 30 Minutes or Less
Easy Cottage Cooking
Essential Barbecue
Essential Salads
Fish & Seafood
Healthy Family Meals
Make It Ahead!
Make It Chocolate!
Mediterranean Flavours
One Dish Favourites
Pasta & Noodles
Quick 400-Calorie Favourites
Sweet & Simple

The Affordable Feasts Collection
The Appetizer Collection
The Barbecue Collection
The International Collection
The One Dish Collection
The Slow Cooker Collection
The Vegetarian Collection

canadianliving.com/books